Gail Styles is a mother of three, living in Hampshire and a retired special needs learning support assistant. She is excited about her newfound love of writing and the possibilities of where it will take her. When not writing, she enjoys walking, trying to stay fit, socialising with family and friends and travelling.

For my three amazing children, Cheryl, Phil and Liv. Live your life no matter what.

Gail Styles

CANCER – V – MND

AUSTIN MACAULEY PUBLISHERS®
LONDON * CAMBRIDGE * NEW YORK * SHARJAH

All of the events in this memoir are true to the best of author's memory. The views expressed in this memoir are solely those of the author.

A CIP catalogue record for this title is available from the British Library.

ISBN 9781035883691 (Paperback)
ISBN 9781035883714 (ePub e-book)
ISBN 9781035883707 (Audiobook)

www.austinmacauley.com

First Published 2025
Austin Macauley Publishers Ltd®
1 Canada Square
Canary Wharf
London
E14 5AA

Table of Contents

What a Year and Beyond

So, who am I? I'm Gail, mum of 3 to Cheryl, Phil and Liv, Nana to Joshua, Reuben (angel grandbaby) and Annabelle, and wife to Pete. We have a cat called Snowbell and a fish who is so old I'm surprised it is still here and won't have any other fish in the tank so I'm guessing it prefers its own company. I am a learning support assistant at a special needs school and this is my journey over the last couple of years.

The start of 2020 was so promising, a 50th birthday to celebrate, an 18th birthday, our youngest Liv heading to university in September and the decision to downsize our house to move nearer to the sea. Then, this thing called Covid hit and everything went weird.

Hubby, whose 50th we were celebrating went off for a long boozy weekend to Tenerife with his mates, a hairy few days (but enjoyable I believe) of wondering if they were going to make it home as not only us but the whole world was plunged into lockdown.

The family holiday to Turkey was well and truly cancelled and our intended house move sort of stumbled. Our house was put on the market with lots of restrictions around viewing as and when they were allowed.

Our house hunting was also made harder as we couldn't travel very much so we had to do a lot of online looking, which isn't quite the same. Considering we knew roughly where we wanted to move to, we couldn't find anything we liked and had to broaden our area quite considerably.

Pete's 50th birthday came and went, sadly a very low-key affair as no travelling or family were allowed to visit, we postponed celebrations until things were more normal.

Liv was diagnosed with Autism (not something we were surprised about) at the end of May, literally a couple of weeks before her 18th birthday, due to this fact and COVID all the promises of support we were given never materialised as she left the child services and joined the big world of adulthood.

Liv's birthday was quite low-key but at least family were able to visit and she could enjoy a small celebration, again proper celebrations at a later date.

Pete was working from home during the pandemic and I was still going to work, different hours and less children in the classes, very surreal and strange times. I went out walking for our allowed exercise times and Pete would go running on his own, or with people from his running club as and when restrictions allowed.

I've had bowel issues for a few years, so it wasn't unusual for me to suddenly need a poo when out for my walk. For Pete, working from home was a great advantage as I'd sometimes need a lift home very quickly (public loos or shop toilets were closed).

As the school year came to a close, I decided I needed to sort out my tummy issues and did an E-consult with my doctor, as you couldn't actually get to see a doctor due to the COVID restrictions. Pete had been out running and had a couple of falls/stumbles and his right foot was dragging a little, so he decided he'd get that checked out around the same time.

I was asked to get some blood taken and a few days later whilst sitting in the vets waiting for the cat to have her overdue yearly booster and check-up I got a weird call from my doctor, basically saying, I'm really sorry you have a blood infection and a consultant from haematology will be in touch very soon, it was obviously serious and scared the shite out of me.

What on Earth do you do when you're in the middle of the vet's waiting room but wait for the cat (we weren't allowed in the consultation room due to restrictions), put a smile on my face, act normally, pay the bill and get in the car.

In shock, I drove home thinking I couldn't talk to Pete he was working and had travelled a few hours away (you were allowed at this point to be driving places), he wasn't due back until early evening, and I couldn't talk to the kids as I needed to talk to Pete first.

So, I messaged my friend, Donna, and she came straight round and I just sobbed on her shoulder, I had no idea what was going on but it didn't sound good and I was scared.

I managed to get through the day and just when Pete was home Cheryl phoned for a chat to see how things were, there's nothing like trying to act normally but wanting to get your daughter off of the phone without being rude or arousing her suspicions that something was wrong.

Eventually, I blurted out to Pete about the phone call, I was sobbing so much he couldn't understand a word I'd said, but there was the big hug I needed to feel reassured and safe.

Once I'd calmed down, we managed to talk, obviously, the word cancer was mentioned, but at this point, we had no idea what was wrong and almost like a sixth sense Cheryl phoned back. We did talk to the kids but as I didn't know much at this stage, there wasn't much to say.

Two days later, I had a call from a very nice consultant from haematology, he explained that my blood results indicated I had an infection, which could be cancer or if not it was pre-cancer. Over the next few weeks, I had blood tests, and a bone marrow biopsy, which involved collecting some of my bone marrow and a slither of bone from my hip (this wasn't painful but the weird sensation and noise as the bone sample was collected wasn't very nice).

I wanted to see what was collected and was also shown the tool used to get the bone sample, it looked very much like an apple core and I'm glad I didn't see it beforehand. Next, was a full body scan, I was to be in the machine for over an hour as they scanned every part of me.

I was told I would be asked to hold my breath for a few seconds and this would be at the end of the procedure. Never having had this sort of scan before I was extremely apprehensive, trying to get on the bed part with your dignity intact and wearing a hospital gown is no mean feat, my hip was still sore from the biopsy which didn't help.

A cage-type mask thing was placed over my head and face, in my mind I was actually thinking I'm not sure I can do this, breathe. I'm telling myself to calm down (so glad I've been to yoga and remembered the breathing), and a pair of headphones were placed over my head.

I, obviously, have a small head as the ear bits were in fact halfway down my cheeks, they asked what music I'd like…a bit of Keane, it might help calm me, they also said, if I couldn't cope or needed to stop, just say, as they could see and hear me, not exactly reassuring.

In I was slid, it scared the life out of me, I'd rather have more bone marrow biopsies than this, the clattering of the machine was so loud and I could only just hear the music. I kept breathing slowly and remembering a beach holiday abroad, and then I felt the presence of my granddad over my left shoulder.

Whether you believe in the spirit world or not, I do (and at this moment it's what I need), I felt very calm, it seemed like no time at all and I was being asked to hold my breath for short periods, the ordeal was nearly over. I must admit to shedding a few tears as I dressed and headed out to Pete.

As I was having my tests, Pete was also having scans and blood tests, he had to go to Reading for one of his scans, so we had a little walk along the river, grabbed a sandwich and sat watching boats going along the Thames, very calming in a very topsy turvy time.

I received an appointment for what was originally a phone consultation, which was then changed to a face-to-face appointment for 24 August, it wasn't looking good in my mind as anything face-to-face with a medical professional was rare, but I shouldn't jump to conclusions.

Pete was allowed to come with me, thankfully (still, so many restrictions around COVID) the waiting room was quite empty, guessing most consultations were taking place over the phone, and everyone wearing face masks we were ushered into an office.

Dr Noel introduced himself and there was also a haematology nurse present, I remember feeling quite calm, then there it was, I'm really sorry to tell you, you have multiple myeloma (it's a type of bone marrow cancer), at this point, I felt like I was in the room but not in the room. It is life-limiting (around 10–15 years but with technology and research life expectancy has already increased from what it used to be). It is treatable but not curable.

Dr Noel had expected me to be in the pre-cancerous stage, where I would need to be monitored but not receive treatment. Sadly, the results of my test said differently, but it had been caught early.

There were some holes in my bones, in my spine, hips and chest area (apparently, if not detected early enough, it would have affected my spine possibly causing it to crumble and I'd have ended up in a wheelchair), which with treatment won't get worse but won't repair themselves either.

I was given booklets on the condition, treatment and all the medication it would involve and also a follow-up appointment to go through my treatment plan. I was also told it wouldn't be safe for me to return to my job, so was given a sick note to sign me off work for the next six months.

It's funny, how automatic pilot kicks in, we made our way back to the car park, gripping each other's hand but not saying a word, all I could think of was shit we've got to tell the kids. Pete went to pay for the parking, and by the time he got back to the car tears were streaming down my face, he got in the car, and we just held each other and sobbed.

Pulling ourselves together, we went home to talk to the kids who were waiting for us, not something any parent really wanted to do.

I had a follow-up appointment to go over my treatment plan, which would start after I'd seen a dentist, as part of my treatment would involve a bone-strengthening infusion, just in case, I needed to have a troublesome tooth removed.

At this point, we finally sold our house (just what we needed), we had been advised by Dr Noel that Basingstoke was the best place for my treatment and was concerned that if we moved away, it could affect my treatment plan or add travelling time to treatments.

With that in mind, the fact Pete was having physio, still had no diagnosis and his symptoms were getting worse (he was wobbly on his legs and his hands shook if holding or trying to carry anything) we decided to downsize and look for somewhere local.

My treatment was due to start on 15 September, it was a six-month plan with chemo injections every week, monthly bone-strengthening injections and a lot of medication (steroids, antibiotics, blood thinning injections, thalidomide, calcium and vitamin D).

After that, they would be harvesting my bone marrow in readiness for a bone marrow transplant in Southampton Hospital, monthly blood tests and catch-ups with Dr Noel were also in the mix. Before then and after my dental appointment, we decided to go spend a few days in Bournemouth.

It was just what we needed, a few days relaxing by the sea, but it also showed how much Pete was struggling, how far he couldn't walk and he couldn't carry anything or hold anything in his hands without his hands shaking.

Considering only a few months before, he'd been out regularly running with buddies from his running club (when he was able to due to COVID) or on his own, he regularly ran

5Ks and 10Ks and has a host of medals to show off his achievements.

It helped to keep him fit and sound-minded, and he enjoyed the comradery of the group he ran with within the club. At this moment, he had no idea if or when, he'd be able to go out running with them again.

I decided that to help with my well-being to write a blog about the journey during my treatment, this was about me and I never included what was going on with Pete or anything else (he was paying for physio to help with his mobility).

Feelings
14/09/2020

It's been seven *weeks since I had a seemingly innocent blood test, and three weeks since my diagnosis. In the weeks of tests and waiting, I felt more anxious, worried, scared and didn't sleep very well.*

After the initial shock of finding out I have Myeloma, I feel strangely calm, I've had tears (especially when I read the little card I have to carry around with me once my treatment starts stating I have to go straight to the hospital and be put on antibiotics if I get certain symptoms), felt sad, very out of my depth, scared, worried for my family, but mainly apprehensive.

I cried when my grandson put the 'This is My Fight' song on the blog and actually cried tears of happiness when we sold our house and our youngest passed her theory test. I've never thought why me, why not me or it's not fair. It is what it is and I need to deal with it as best I can, with positivity and a smile on my face.

If I can cope, so will my family and friends. Once my treatment starts, I'm hoping the apprehension will ease. I'll know exactly what I'm dealing with and how my body is going to cope with it. There are going to be bumps along the way, but that's fine, I'll deal with them as they arise.

This has sidestepped our intended plans, so we've had to adapt and go with the flow of what needs to be, rather than what was going to be. I have had so much love and support from family, friends and people I don't really know, to each and every one of you, Thank You. It is very humbling, very much appreciated and helps to make the journey a little easier.

Hubby and I have had a few days away in Bournemouth, in my mind, there is nothing more therapeutic than the sound of waves. We sat by the sea, chilled, when it got busy we retired to our hotel room which had an amazing view of the pier and sea, and people watched from a safe distance.

We got food delivered to the hotel, so didn't even have to leave our room. Just what we needed. I'm very chilled and relaxed, ready for the start of my treatment tomorrow.

My First Treatment
15/09/2020

Last night, I had a lovely catch-up and chill time with some of my besties. It took my mind off of today and I was totally fine all evening until just before we were leaving I was asked so how are you really. That was it, flood gates opened and I cried (my emotions take me by surprise at times), couldn't even have hugs as have to social distance.

This morning, before leaving for the hospital, a friend popped by for a cuppa...nice and kept my mind occupied. To be fair the hospital was far easier than I anticipated, bone-strengthening IV meds and a chemo jab to the stomach were a piece of cake compared to goodness knows what I was thinking.

I'm going to be taught how to give myself the chemo jab, then I'll only need to go to the hospital once a month. Then, I was given the bag of meds to bring home. Oh my goodness, talk about confusing me.

Once home, I sit, read and start taking the meds, then I have to give myself the blood thinning jab into my stomach, talked through by hubby, done, go me. At this point, I started to feel a little spaced out and teary, too many meds close together.

My sister called, and whilst talking she said, I wasn't making much sense and said I'd call her tomorrow. A little cat nap was needed, so I napped. I set a timer for 7 pm to remind me to take the last meds of the day, which is supposed to make me sleepy, we'll see.

Tomorrow will be easier; I'll be able to space out the meds.

Thank you for all the love and support I received today. It truly helps and as always I am very humbled. I know, it's not my saying but I'm using it.

It is okay not to be okay, but I will be okay.

As I started my treatment, our hunt for a new home started, a skip was ordered and with the help of the kids the attic was cleared. I don't know to this day, what was actually up there and if there was anything, I might have wanted to keep but it was completely emptied, the skip was well and truly full up and can't say I've missed anything.

Obviously, not everything was binned, so the boxing up of our belongings began. At this point, Pete was able to help pack and with care, we could carry things together out into the garage.

He was still undergoing physio but no further appointments seemed forthcoming about possible diagnoses or reasons for what was happening to him.

MND was mentioned in passing to him, and when he told me, we looked at each other and both said, "Nah, it couldn't be."

I laughed as I said, "That would mean you'd get sicker than me!"

Relaxed
20/09/2020

What a great weekend, started with going to the loo, yeah, I had a poo (bowel movement) or two, was less tired and didn't feel sick (always a bonus). Had an unexpected socially distanced visit from my grown-up daughter and granddaughter (both have sniffles) bearing McDonald's breakfast (yummy and thank you) was so lovely to see them.

A full-on day of house hunting, a stop off at the Portsmouth Arms market (would be rude not to stop for a quick drink whilst there), so we sat in the sun people watching before I had to go get my flu jab. With all this excitement you'd think I'd be exhausted, nope, not even after taking my evening medication.

I had one of those weird night sleeps where I wasn't clock watching but I wasn't in a full deep sleep, not helped by the cat on the bed, off the bed, on the bed off the bed.

Finally, after the cat sat on my chest and proceeded to purr very loudly, I got up and made myself a cuppa, it was 5:30 am, for goodness sake. Hubby was also awake, so, I put the TV on and watched a Harry Potter movie, he fell asleep I didn't.

I know, I was not quite there emotionally when I cried at the death of Sirius Black it really, never happened before, but I'm sure it will again. A visit from my sister, then brother and sister-in-law made my morning, so lovely to see them, but so, so, miss having hugs.

Yes, I'm tired and a little washed out, bemused by the almost pulled muscle ache in my right side and soreness across my shoulders, is the medication working, I really don't know, is it something I'm going to have to get used to?

I hope not, and at this point in time, I know so little, I'm just learning as I go along. Hubby has dinner cooking in the slow cooker, the sun is shining, it is okay not to be okay and right now, I am okay.

Week 1 Done
22/09/2020

Where on Earth has that last week gone? 1 down 27 more weeks to go.

Yesterday, apart from a little tiredness, was a really good day, went to the shop with hubby, and sat in the sunshine, really mundane stuff, but it makes such a difference when you feel okay whilst doing it.

This morning realised my steroid pills make me feel like yuk, had to take some sickness meds and my head feels all woolly *I think is the best way to describe it. I've noticed, I'm getting a bit cranky with hubby (he's at the gym having some well-deserved time out), not intentionally, but can't seem to help it (did warn him about the possibility of bitchy wife making an appearance) and I may use that excuse if he annoys me!*

So, second trip to Winchester, literally went in had my chemo jab and back out again. Thankfully, I've been on all meds for a week now, so didn't need to come home and shove a load in at once. Maybe, that's why I don't feel as bad as I did last week or as emotional.

I am sore and a bit weary, have pottered a bit, but mainly chilled and had a good natter on the phone with a friend.

It's okay not to be okay, today I'm doing okay.

Head Down
27/09/2020

So, it's been a few days and apart from having a good Wednesday, where I was able to drive youngest to work and do a bit of shopping, I've felt like poop and really struggled. Only to be expected I tell myself, but honestly, I had no idea what to expect and don't like it at all.

I had a surprise package through the post on Thursday (thank you so much Sharon Webster), really put a smile on my face and brought home to me how much everyone's love and support mean to me and is so much needed.

I again have had constipation since I had the chemo jab, did get something from the chemist and the situation eased Friday morning. The fatigue, woolly head and sickness stayed till yesterday midday and I spent all day Friday in my PJs, too tired to do anything but frustrated with myself for feeling like this (I know should give myself a break).

My back hurts/aches, the top of my neck aches. What on Earth is going on with my body? I seem to have no control over what goes on where, as for wind, all I can say is thank goodness hubby loves me, never knew so much wind could come out of seemingly nowhere.

I now have the added pain and discomfort of a swollen knee. I think it's some sort of fluid retention but has resulted in a call to 111 this morning just to be on the safe side. A phone call and then a video call have given me some relief that it isn't anything too major, keep an eye on it and I have a call with Dr Noel tomorrow, so will check it out with him.

It is hopefully something to do with the meds I'm on (not anything arthritic-related) and will sort itself out with the help of an ice pack and paracetamol.

I'm not feeling sorry for myself, far from it, just struggling big time to adjust to what is my new normal and dragging my complaining body with me. I miss the routine of work, speaking to people, seeing friends being part of normality (whatever that is at the moment).

Being able to do what I want, when I want, my life was so different at the moment. Yes, I'm struggling, but I'll get there, I just need to let myself know it's okay not to be okay, that I'm going to be okay.

We've found a house, not what I thought we'd end up getting but weirdly the one Pete said all along he liked, it had no garage and the stairs were in the living room, things I'd not wanted, but when we went for the first viewing it just felt right, you know when you know.

We took Liv for a look on our second viewing, then put in an offer, a little bit of haggling and the house was ours. Thank goodness, no more viewings. I was struggling to cope and it was one less thing for us to worry about. Now, for the downsizing, we were moving from a four-bed to a three-bed house, smaller in every aspect, selling, giving away and a good sort out was the order of the day.

Week 2 Done
29/09/2020

Yesterday was a much better day, the swelling on my knee went down and I could actually weigh bare on it. A call from Dr Noel brought some really positive news, my bad blood count is down. One week in, and the treatment is already doing its job. Dr Noel was really pleased and so am I.

My woolly brain is really evident at the moment, last week I put one1 week done 27 to go! I'm only supposed to be having 24 weeks of treatment, where 27 came from I do not know, 24-1=23, so now it's two 2 weeks done, 22 weeks to go.

Everyone's, love, support, messages and continued offer of help never ceases to amaze me. I can't put into words how much it means to me and helps me. More wonderful gifts, from the lovely Donna and Louisa, snugly PJs, fluffy bed socks and scented candles. Thank you so much.

My chemo jab today was actually quite sore and the meds have given me thrush, other than that, all is good. Couldn't believe the price I had to pay in the chemist for medication for it (yes, I could have got in on a prescription but don't know how long I would have waited).

It didn't stop me from coming home and taking myself out for a mile-and-a-quarter walk in the sun was shining it was great to be out, it might have taken me 40 minutes (a couple of weeks ago, that would have been almost three miles), with wobbly legs and stiff knees, I did it.

I need to try to get myself out every day, even if it's just around the block, then, it will be easier and I'll be quicker. I am tired, and my tummy is sore, but today, it's okay not to be okay, I am okay.

I'm Good
02/10/2020

My treatment this week hasn't (so far) floored me as much as it did last week. Yes, I'm constipated, eased with a little help from a laxative, and my thrush has settled down. I didn't sleep from 3 am on Tuesday morning until Wednesday night and bounced through the day.

I still have terrible wind (for which, I keep apologising to hubby) and yesterday afternoon exhaustion overtook me. I even had to have a little nap which I don't usually do. I'm not quite as emotional and not as moody (not sure if hubby would agree on this). I know each day is different, how I feel and how my body is reacting, and I am learning to listen to my body, no matter how frustrating I find it. At the moment, I am good.

Week 3
06/10/2020

So, week 3 is done. 21 more weeks to do, seems such a long time, but baby steps, each day then each week, it'll be done in no time.

My chemo jab, for some reason, was particularly painful, but saying that so was my blood test, different people seem to hurt more in their execution of a needle than others. I have a rather nasty bruise on my arm and just the normal bruising on my stomach.

I haven't felt quite as tired or emotional or sick, no thrush and the laxative medication is helping over this last week (still have the crying for no reason, usually when I'm tired or hubby has said something I took offence to but he didn't mean it how I took it).

It's been great to see my brother, sister and bro-in-law, son and partner, share in my grandson's 12th birthday celebrations and catch up with friends. Not altogether, not on the same day and the six people's rule was never broken! (just in case, anyone thought I might have broken the rules)

Some more lovely gifts, thank you, Karen and Andy, Margaret and Dave, Mike and Lyns. I know I say it a lot, but people's love support and kindness are helping me through this. COVID is not and I miss all those extra hugs I could/should be having but daren't.

Not so good was the swelling of my left leg over the weekend, couldn't bear weight, or bend it. It was extremely swollen, so sore and has kept me awake for the last two nights. So tonight, I'm hoping (very shortly) to be going to sleep and sleeping through the night, fingers crossed.

I saw a doctor whilst at the hospital today, they think it may be related to the steroids I'm taking, typically by the time I got to the hospital, the swelling had substantially reduced and I had a lot more movement in my knee.

The outcome was to monitor my knee, call the emergency number if it becomes a problem for me and the Dr will check on me next week. Tonight, I can bear weight on it, walk normally and go up/down the stairs like a normal person, happy days.

Yes, my back still gives me pain but I've learnt to adjust and change how I sit or lay to minimise this. It is still early days, I've a lot to learn and adjust to but I'm getting there, my frustration at things I can't do but should be able to do means I adapt, rest and do whatever it takes to get me to where I want to be or what I want to do.

I hadn't given a thought about the use of my normal body products, but guess I should be checking out what is best for my body with all the medication being put into it. I read in one of the leaflets about using kind products for my hair, so had sorted something with the help of a friend and my hairdresser (thanks Kirsty).

Funny, how I just don't think about some things, but do others, there again, I do have a foggy brain most of the time (that's my excuse and I'm sticking to it), it's almost as bad as when I had the kids and couldn't remember anything. I am now off to bed; I am okay, in fact, I am good.

As my treatment progressed, it was quite apparent how much Pete was being affected by whatever was wrong with him. Much as I would've liked a cuppa and even a slice of toast in bed in the mornings I felt like poo, Pete was unable to carry anything up the stairs. It took all his concentration to get himself safely up them, never mind anything else.

We even invested in a posh kettle thing to keep in our bedroom along with all the stuff needed so we could have hot drinks upstairs (neither of us had milk in our drinks so it wasn't an issue).

His right side seemed to be more problematic than his left. Pete got a left-handed mouse to help him keep using his computer as he was still working and very much against his will, a walking stick was purchased, it was either that and help himself, or fall over.

Liv also went off to uni, luckily, it wasn't far, but Cheryl had to help move her in as neither Pete nor myself could carry anything and due to the pandemic only one person was able to go in the building with her. Thankfully, it was a good call as the lift was out of order and Liv's room was up three flights of stairs!

Liv was also having driving lessons each week and was near enough for us to go collect her to enable her to continue with them. It also meant, the transition of leaving home was more manageable for Liv as she was able to frequently come home and we could go visit her if need be.

I rarely drove at this point as my meds often left me woolly-headed, thankfully, Pete was still able to drive and collect Liv as and when required, and drove me to my treatment in Winchester each week.

Finally, Some Sleep
10/10/2020

After three nights, with next to no sleep (Tuesday night, I was watching Polar Express at 2 am!) I slept for seven *hours on Wednesday night, in pure bliss.*

Wednesday, as seems to be a regular occurrence, I was buzzing around and as the week progressed, my energy levels have slowly run out. My chemo belly seemed extra big this week at one point, I looked like I was due to give birth with the added bonus of constipation my poor stomach or clothes didn't stand a chance and resulted in even my looser clothes struggling to cover me up.

I had to, of course, resort to good old comfy PJs bottoms. My knee has been sore all week and is starting to swell again, so I'm trying to be a little more mobile (even though I really can't be arsed today) to see if it helps.

I've also been helping my youngest to pack up her room ready for uni and yesterday, we deposited one happy young adult at her chosen university. I'm so proud of how she has handled the last few months, it's certainly not been easy and now, she starts on the next chapter of her life and I hope she has a ball.

For me it's the first time, I'll be child-free in a long, long time will I miss her?

Week 4 Done 13/10/2020

4 weeks done, 20 more to do, first round of treatment finished, second round started today.

So, what have I learnt? I'm full of wind most of the time, constipated, emotional and can cry for no apparent reason. I get irritated easily, again for no apparent reason, my stomach is bloated/fat most of the time, my hair is thinning, wearing a bra hurts, and wearing nice knickers is out of the question as they roll down (thankfully, they don't fall down) so its big knickers all day every day.

I feel sick a few days of the week, I'm tired but can't sleep properly. I'm a pain in the arse to live with, my back hurts, my knees hurt and I get very frustrated with myself when I struggle to do what I would normally do. I miss hugs (air hugs are just not the same) and being able to go out and about wherever, whenever.

I am learning to listen to my body because if I don't I'll suffer. I am learning to adapt to what I can do and to relax more.

I've learnt what an amazing bunch of people I have around me, from my so supportive (suffering) hubby who will do anything he can to ease my pain and make me feel better, my kids (who always tell me to stop doing so much and maybe, I am finally starting to listen), close family friends and people I don't know very well, the love, support, offers of help and gifts have been truly overwhelming, humbling and lovely. It really picks me up when I see the messages and support on my blog.

Today, I am tired from my treatment, my knee hasn't stopped hurting (which I'm hoping with the medication supplied will now be sorted), I have the shakes and my stomach is sore. It is nothing I can't cope with and I count myself lucky, I can do this, and I will do this (too many people to kick my arse and keep me on track)

Some girlfriends are coming over for a much-needed catch-up later (socially distanced and not breaking the rule of six). I have this. Today, I am good.

Week 5 Done
21/10/2020

5 weeks finished, 19 more to do, two infusions done, so only four more to do and I can't believe it's been over a week since I last posted.

I had a lovely catch-up with the girls last Tuesday and, a good Wednesday, then, it all went pear-shaped. I felt so tired, ached and the pain in my knee, warm baths and hot water bottle eased it but didn't take it away.

I was very emotional (thanks hubby for all the cuddles) and just slept, with a constant fuzzy head and inability to focus on anything. It took until yesterday morning to wake up and feel a little normal, well normal for me anyway. In short, the infusion is a necessity, but I don't like how it knocks me out and makes me feel.

Me being me, my eldest was coming to lunch with the grandkids on Saturday, even though I was all over the place, I thought it would be a good idea to bake a cake. So, I pulled the food mixer out of the cupboard and dropped it, how it missed my bare feet I do not know, the bonus was that it still worked and the cake turned out okay.

It was lovely to spend time with them, even if I was there in body but certainly not mind.

I thought my hair was thinning out quite a lot, but it turns out, it isn't as bad as I thought, my hair has changed colour, becoming much lighter at the front (no not grey yet) and blonder with a hint of silver, in fact it looks like I've had highlights.

So, thank you Kirsty for that reassurance and ways you'll be able to change my hair to cover up the thinness at the front, if need be. Can't beat a haircut to make you feel better.

Then, an added bonus, the doorbell goes and hubby got someone to make me a dairy-free cake, it looked and tasted amazing, thank you. You certainly know how to put a smile on my face, love you so much.

I was expecting the meds I've been given for gout to have started working, obviously, it hasn't. So, I asked the nurse whilst I was having my jab about them. I had the foresight to take a photo of the pill packet as I can't remember anything at the moment (which I'm assured by the nurse is quite normal), apparently it takes two to three weeks for that medication to kick in, that's fine, I now know it will get easier with time.

Apart from no sleep until 4 am last night. (I resorted to a sleepy-time podcast, I don't actually think I heard more than the first few lines and I was gone.) Shame, I woke up when it finished an hour and a half later, could have done with a few more hours, but some is better than none fingers crossed, for a decent sleep tonight.

Couldn't even blame the cat as the youngest was home for the night ready for a driving lesson this morning, so the cat went into her room instead of ours (then decided to come to join me downstairs, the cat that is not the daughter).

In a nutshell, the last week has been shite, but I'm through it now, I am learning to listen to my body and when it tells me to sleep or rest, I do it isn't worth the suffering it can cause if I continue to push myself, even though it frustrates the hell out of me.

I wasn't okay but I am now, and the good thing is, if you see me out and about I look healthy and normal, thanks to my chemo glow.

Whilst at the uni, I took an early phone call from Dr Noel. (he did say he might call early, but I thought that would be earlier Monday morning not Friday instead!) It turns out, that my blood has dropped to a nearer normal level (normal for me), as I near the end of my first round of treatment.

My body has responded fantastically to all that has been thrown at it and Dr Noel is really pleased as I am. He did mention that my knee problem could be some form of gout, which is quite common apparently with the meds I'm taking so, in my pill bag next week will be some medication to hopefully, help settle it, my fingers are crossed.

I'm now going to put my feet up (keeping mobile has had it for today) and veg in front of the TV.

Today, I am tired but I am good.

Week 6 Done
28/10/2020

6 weeks done, 18 more to go and I'm a quarter of the way through my treatment. Treatment wasn't until 5:30 pm, it felt very late and I was tired before I even got to the hospital. It was quieter and I was in and out within 20 minutes, with hardly any waiting time.

During the last week, I've had visits from friends, and family, with a first takeout from the Portsmouth Arms (it was very nice too), lots of lovely gifts, a homemade Bakewell tart and the amazing love and support from everyone never ceases to humble and amaze me.

It really gives me a boost. I can never thank everyone enough or put into words, how much it means to me. I received a lovely hamper from my class on Friday, it has been sat on the kitchen side for me to admire, youngest came home yesterday, tells me to open it so she can see what's in it, inside, which I didn't realise were some lovely artwork and messages from the children in the class, bought a tear to my eye and made me feel very appreciated, even though, I've not worked with them yet this school year.

So, how have I been? Wednesdays continue to be my best day even with little sleep, my knees were still bad but not as painful, it was constipation that got me this week. Three and a half days without going for a poo, my stomach was in agony and cramped up if I ate or drank anything.

This wasn't good as we were invited to neighbours for dinner, due to my normal dietary issues, I was made a separate curry containing everything that was safe for me to eat, lovely as it was I could only eat a small token amount due to the pain.

I was straight home to bed, with peppermint tea, paracetamol and a hot water bottle. I was an emotional wreck most of the weekend, so hubby was in overdrive with his hugs and cuddles. First thing Monday morning, I emailed Victoria, the haematology nurse for some advice. I'm now taking Movicol with the hope that I never have a repeat of last weekend.

It's funny how different issues seem to appear each week for me to deal with and find a solution for. I am hoping that the majority have now come to light and I know what I'm dealing with, but who knows what may crop up as long as I listen to my body, take advice when needed and also try to source my own solutions, everything will be fine.

I've also realised being diagnosed with cancer during the pandemic is a very lonely, isolating time, normally, I'm guessing you would be able to talk to other people going through the same thing and find out who is receiving treatment for the same cancer.

It is not the case, we all wear masks and sit socially distanced to receive our treatment, we may nod at each other but certainly don't talk to each other. I'm glad I chose not to give myself the chemo jab.

At least, I can ask the nurse questions and concerns I may have, see a doctor if need be and not feel quite so isolated or on my own for the medical side of things.

I'm doing okay, I deal with the challenges cancer throws at me, and I will win.

The survey has been done on our house and Pete has had a spine MRI, a little progress in both areas.

Week 7 Done
03/11/2020

Week 7 done. 17 more to go, time goes so quickly when you're having fun!

The last week started brilliantly, great days Wednesday and Thursday, despite still not sleeping Tuesday night, was able to shop, potter and feel almost normal. I loved it and did listen when my body told me it had had enough.

Despite being on Movicol, I still had constipation, Friday night and most of Saturday the stomach cramps were awful, it didn't last long, but the cramping continued into Monday, my appetite vanished and I struggled to drink anything, which then added to the constipation issue, fingers crossed it will be a better outcome this week.

My knees are still stiff but I have been mobile all the time which is an improvement and my head has been a little clearer. Still, can't remember anything, repeat myself continuously and have felt really irritated for the last couple of days, at TV programmes and over nothing in particular, who knows what that's about.

As my hair is slowly falling out, I cannot help but marvel at the fact my lip and chin hair appears to be getting a life of its own. I know, we ladies of a certain age can be plagued with this sort of thing, but it hasn't affected me to date. Now, I find myself having to yank out wire-like hairs seemingly like every few days, there again as I wear a face mask out nobody would know if I develop a moustache or little beard because you can't see it, so does it really matter?

It does to me, so I'll continue to yank them out, which is probably making them grow even more, no win situation, but it makes me feel I'm winning the battle. Had a visit from my son and partner on Saturday was lovely to see them but I did sadly keep falling asleep during their visit, which was a shame.

Sunday, a visit from my eldest and the grandkids, so love the ability of kids to carry on normally, messing around, being noisy, just being them and I even managed to stay awake the whole time.

I watched some of the Pride of Britain awards at the weekend, and what other people go through helps keep my battle in perspective, people like Liz C, with her help and guidance, is one very inspirational lady.

Still, the love, support and messages from everyone amaze me and keep me going, as we go into lockdown again, those video calls from whatever app is used will be my window to the outside world my social interaction, my lifeline to something that is so not normal, not only in my little world but the whole world. Be kind to each other, and look out for each other, we need each other. Short-term pain for long-term gain.

After much pinging between Southampton and Basingstoke Hospitals, Pete finally got to see a consultant on 9 November and got the diagnosis he certainly didn't want to hear and neither did I. Yes, he has Motor Neurones Disease. What a load of shit.

That and the fact it was very life-limiting was about all the info I was able to take in. Once again, we had to break the news to our kids, then family and friends, believe me, it wasn't any easier the second time around.

I didn't want to read up too much or hear about it, I wasn't ready to know about what lay ahead of us.

Pete was signed off work and had to have a conversation with his boss and make arrangements to have his company car picked up. At this point, he was struggling to get in his work car anyway, but could still manage our car as it was bigger and higher up which was easier for him.

After struggling with her driving, Liv changed to learning in an automatic, within weeks she'd mastered it and put in for a driving test, the test was due to be taken in November. Surprise, it was cancelled at the last minute and postponed until July!

Week 8 Done 11/11/2020

8 weeks done, one-third of my way through treatment, 16 more weeks to go and the third cycle started yesterday.

I came home from treatment, shattered, my arm was sore and so was my back. I have learnt I get so much achiness/soreness from the infusion for the first few days, a hot water bottle across my back does wonders and paracetamol for the pain helps.

On a very positive note, felt really good last week, with no constipation (yeah), so no stomach cramping, just tiredness, still have a stiff knee and my stubbly chin, all small things.

My son and youngest daughter surprised me with a visit on my birthday last Wednesday (was good, to actually be awake to talk to my son), my eldest daughter had a sore throat so sadly couldn't join us.

I had a great day, lots of lovely messages, cards and gifts. I felt very loved and I very much appreciate everyone taking their time to think of me and it was lovely to see people before going into lockdown again.

A phone call from Dr Noel on Friday confirmed my blood levels are now normal (some light levels that were over 200 at the beginning of treatment are down to 6.9, have no idea what they are only the results are great). I am on a list for Southampton, just waiting for communication from them for the bone marrow harvesting, hopefully, I'll hear soon.

Quite emotional today, maybe, due to tiredness, although for the first time on a Tuesday since I started treatment, I managed to stay in bed all night and had three to four hours of sleep, go me. When I cry at stupid things on the TV or cry because someone else is crying I know the meds are messing with my emotions.

Learn I'm also getting a bit clumsy, I dropped a plate on my foot (luckily, it didn't break, my foot or the plate) leaving a nice bruise and then I smacked my arm on a door handle, another bruise and yes, I cried both times, but it did hurt both times, so I'm saying it was acceptable to cry.

Things seem to have settled into a sort of pattern, the infusion messes with me big time, causing me discomfort and pain. By the end of the second week, things seem to settle and everything becomes easier. Yes, I get tired, so I sleep when I need to, some days I'm hungry, some days I'm not and I need to drink plenty of fluids.

This I struggle with but do force myself to drink (this is where I miss my green tea with lemon, could drink loads of it, but it messes with some of the medication, so can't have it). I get hot flushes, haven't yet worked out if it's the steroids or chemo as have both around the same time.

At the end of the last two weeks, I've actually felt really good, once the fuzzy head has settled, which can be any time up to midday and I've felt almost normal. I still can't concentrate on anything, or remember anything, a magazine seems to be my reading limit at the moment and I can't even manage a puzzle.

So, lots of TV and films it is. I listen to my body, which means, I don't get into meltdown mode with the pain I've caused myself. Such an improvement from the first cycle of treatment.

This week is good, I am good.

Week 9 Done
17/11/2020

9 down 15 more weeks to go and I was literally in the hospital for 10 minutes, which included temperature and blood pressure checks (did have a little panic when I was told my temp was 37.8, that was with an ear probe, it was double checked under my tongue, 36.4 phew!).

Very emotional last week, with lots of tears, so lots of cuddles were required from hubby (I do get cuddles normally, just sometimes, I need more) achy back, and no constipation, but a bit of a gripey stomach, nothing compared to what I can get so all manageable and still getting pain in my knees.

I can still walk around, climb the stairs, and bend my knees, they just hurt, the meds have definitely helped, just not taken the pain away, good old paracetamol does the trick (good job it does).

I miss seeing my family and friends. Facetime is good but nothing beats seeing/talking to other people face to face (hugging would be even better). Thank you to everyone who takes the time to read my blog, friends and family, and the continued messages, love and support from you all.

It really does mean a lot, it helps keep me focused and staying positive in these weird challenging times. I got the, you are extremely, clinically venerable letter telling me to shield last week, which I was anyway, so anything we need other than food, for the moment comes from Amazon.

It's funny, the things you suddenly need, can't go to a shop to get, so have to turn to deliveries. (Where would we be without modern technology and next-day delivery? Does that make me sound old, well, I am a little bit, so it's acceptable in my eyes).

We took delivery of a new mattress today, it's so high, that my feet don't touch the floor when I sit on the edge of the bed, it makes me feel like the princess from 'The Princess and The Pea' story (for those of you old enough to even remember it).

Fingers crossed for a decent amount of sleep tonight (I have been awake since 3 am, drinking tea at 4 am, back to bed at 4:30 am then dozed for a bit). Life throws challenges at us, it's how we choose to deal with those challenges that counts and in my mind there is always someone worse off.

We need to live life, love life and laugh through life*, it isn't always easy, but it certainly helps, laughter is a good medicine, it's free and gives you less wrinkles than frowning or a sad face (or crying in my case).*

It's been a hard, emotional week, but now, I am good.

Week 10 Done
24/11/2020

10 down 14 more to go, long wait at the hospital today. I was there for nearly an hour just to have my chemo jab; they were so busy and struggling to put everyone somewhere. That's not good in some ways as more people are needing treatment but on the other hand, at least people are getting the treatment needed.

Tuesdays are usually good days, but today wasn't. I haven't been sleeping very well (still getting used to the new mattress) and I've been struggling to drink, possibly the combination has made me very lethargic and teary.

(I hurt my thumb on the ice box of the freezer, thankfully didn't draw blood and it wasn't that sore but I cried, like a baby, resulting in lots of cuddles from hubby, can't beat them to make me feel better.)

I have forced myself to drink which probably means lots of trips to the toilet tonight, but hey, I do feel a little better, early night I think, even if I get a few hours, it'll be better than nothing.

Other than that, I did sleep lots over the weekend, no constipation (yeah), my knee is sore but bearable, the bristles on my chin seem to be behaving themselves, which is more than can be said for the moustache that now seems to be appearing on my upper lip, thank goodness for face masks in some respects no one can see it.

Not that I'm going out anywhere except to the hospital (roll on next week when we can see people) and I have been going out for walks, not very far, but at least I'm out and the weather has been so lovely.

My weight yoyos considerably throughout the week, I just seem to get it back under control, then, I take my steroids again and the cycle repeats. Short-term pain for long-term gain is what I say and obviously the help of my big girl knickers for comfort and keeping wobbly bits in check (which I have called my running shorts as they are so huge).

Tomorrow will be a better day, maybe, I need to listen to my body more and stop my pottering around. I still haven't heard from Southampton about the harvesting of my bone marrow, maybe I just stop worrying about it. It is out of my control and there is nothing I can do about it so I need to let it go.

I have resorted to putting a Christmas tree up and yes, it is early even for me, but nothing beats the twinkling lights to make things feel cosy and better, and no, I haven't got any other decorations up yet, just the tree.

Today, I wasn't okay but I will be. I need to be kinder to myself, just go with the flow and everything will be fine, I will be fine, in fact, I will be good.

Week 11 Done 02/12/2020

11 weeks down, 13 more to go, another long wait yesterday and a very sore administration of my jab, it really stung, to the point of me wanting to jump up and down to take the sting away (when I hurt myself rather than it hurting I get a stinging sensation, I either rub it to take the sting away or shake it out).

It was a later appointment, the hospital appeared quieter, but they were still busy, not quite as long as last week, and got out at 4:20 for a 3:30 pm appointment.

Constipation doesn't seem to be much of a problem any more. I do still take Movicol, as and when I need it, but it appears my body is reverting back to what it used to be, going to the loo loads. I'm surprised, to be honest, the meds didn't affect me more in the beginning.

I certainly didn't like being constipated, not sure why my body can't have a happy medium, but there you go. I did finally settle back into a normal sleep pattern, when I got sleep everything was so much more manageable.

My body is very large *this week; puffy face, and puffy ankles, larger than what is normal for my stomach. I feel a bit like the Michelin tyre man. Hopefully, it'll start reducing tomorrow when the steroids start passing through.*

My knee still gives me trouble, think I'll have to talk to Dr Noel next week about it, nowhere near as bad as the first few weeks, but enough to make me limp about for a few days and interrupt my sleep at night.

I have learnt to do some pottering, then sit down for a while before carrying on, this seems to work and even though I can still get pain in the top of my neck/back and across my shoulders it is nowhere near as bad as when I carry on with what I'm doing regardless.

My emotions are still all over the place, hubby can still look at me, mean nothing by it but I'm crying anyway, but then I do get my bitchy head on and things come out of my mouth that I have no idea where they came from or why or I get very snappy and irritated for no apparent reason. It's a good job he loves me.

Seeing as my fuzzy brain isn't letting me do very much at the moment, I still can't concentrate on anything, so I'm trying audiobooks. It is certainly helping me to sleep!

Don't think I've actually heard a whole chapter yet, it's certainly going to take a while to listen to the book (I've opted for John Green Turtles All The Way Down) with all the going back to hear what I've missed and it's not like I don't have time on my hands anyway.

I am so proud of all my kids, but my youngest has signed up to the Brave the Shave for Macmillan cancer, so very proud of her for taking on this challenge, which means when my hair eventually falls out (I have been assured it will), she will have very little hair, so I will be joining her, rather than her joining me. So, if anyone has a spare few quid, please, support her in this very worthwhile cause.

https://bravetheshave.macmillan.org.uk/shavers/liv-st\les

We come out of lockdown, yeah, I can socially distance and go for a walk with other people, will I still feel isolated, probably, but not as much, especially as I have the ongoing love and support from family and friends and all your positive messages that keep me going no matter how crap I might be feeling. It lifts me up and puts a smile on my face, thank you so much.

Today, I am good.

Week 12 Done
09/12/2020

Week 12 done and dusted halfway through my treatment plan, which means I have jabbed myself 84 times plus 12 chemo jabs, in total so far 96 jabs to my stomach, sometimes, it's not a pretty sight with lots of bruising and other times it's fine, just swollen and wobbly.

As it's said, you can't make an omelette without cracking eggs, a bruised wobbly stomach is a small price to pay for my health. Talking of which, Dr Noel phoned me Thursday afternoon, which totally threw me off, as I was expecting his bit earlier phone call to be on Friday instead of Monday.

He'd got my blood results in and was so, so, pleased, all my markers were still near to normal and one of my light chain levels (no idea what it is or even if I've spelt it right) that was slightly raised has come down to normal.

So yes, I may feel like crap, I may sleep a lot, be constipated or not, have swollen knees, swollen wobbly stomach, feel sick, have to wear big pants, have facial hair issues and have hurting shoulders, neck and back, is it worth it? You bet it's a small price to pay short-term for long-term near normality.

It didn't help either when I was watching TV with hubby the other day he looked over then commented, "Wish I had a tash like that."

What could I say, nothing, seeing as I've mentioned it a few times.

Caught up with my kids (and H) over the weekend (yes, followed the rules it was all as it should have been). Didn't realise how much I missed seeing them, and they brought some normality into the house. With their messing around, it was pure bliss and very much needed, nothing beats having a good laugh and lots of positive input.

Went to the Portsmouth Arms for lunch and, of course, just had to have a look around the market, it's been so long since I've been out anywhere; it felt really weird but also nice to actually be out.

Thank you again, for the ongoing love and support from everyone, the gifts and the people who have sponsored Liv for Brave the Shave, she is well past her target amount, which is amazing and it's such a worthwhile cause.

It's this continued support that helps keep me positive and fighting no matter how rubbish I may be feeling, especially in this very weird, little human-contact world we're in, at the moment.

Remember to live life, love life and laugh, it is okay not to be okay, I am okay.

As we are all too aware, no matter what crap is going on in your own little world, life carries on regardless around you. So, we just got on with life (what else are you supposed to do). Pete went off with Cheryl for a track day he'd got for his birthday, she'd been liaising with them about Pete's decreased mobility, so they were prepared, he had a fantastic day, lots of photos taken, memories made and more importantly, normality.

Our house move is still going ahead but progress was at a painful snail's pace. COVID seemingly causing delays in every aspect. Shopping sprees for a new sofa, bed, mattresses and kitchen table were done and dusted. Thankfully, we were able to continually move delivery dates around as our expected moving date keep being put back.

So much for being in by Christmas, now, I'm left with a dilemma, I always like to put my Christmas tree up at the beginning of December, I'd got a silly little fibre optic one as our tree was already boxed up along with the decorations, so I got a six feet fibre optic one as well. It had to be done; Christmas just isn't Christmas without a decent tree.

Week 13 Done
16/12/2020

13 weeks done, 11 more weeks to go and frustratingly found out yesterday that my treatment is no longer being moved to Basingstoke, for whatever reason, the Rainbow unit is staying at Winchester, would have made it so much easier, but it's not to be.

Usually, when I have my infusion it knocks me out for a few days, it didn't seem to affect me too much until yesterday, I woke up so tired and sore across my back, shoulders and neck and felt sick, so much so I went back to bed mid-morning and slept. It's a good job my treatment was later and I did feel better for it.

So, last week was quite a good week, still had the usual issues around my left knee, had the shakes for a few days, went off my food, and, of course, did have my mood swings poor hubby, he takes it all in his stride and still gives me hugs when I need them.

I actually slept till about 3 am, which is great for a Tuesday night, before going downstairs to watch some movies. Yes. I am tired and still feel a little sick, a dose of my anti-sickness meds should sort that out and I know I can always nap later.

Even though we're out of lockdown, I'm still not going out and about, rarely go into shops and I'm not going anywhere near town. I just don't feel safe around a lot of people and have to protect myself as much as possible. That doesn't mean I don't want to go out.

It's sadly not safe enough yet, hopefully, when more people have had the COVID jab I'll feel safer. Not even sure I can have the jab due to having the stem cell transplant at some point, it will wipe out my immune system completely, which means, it would be a pointless exercise.

I was going to ask Dr Noel about it, but seeing as he caught me unaware with his earlier-than-expected call, I forgot. Not going out much does make me feel very isolated, not being able to see people or have those much-needed hugs is so hard, but it is short-term, so I'll just have to deal with it and make do with Facetime, not the same but, at least, I'm talking to and seeing other people.

That's why everyone's love and support are so important, it lets me know you are there even if I can't see you, and just helps me feel less isolated.

Yes, I am struggling a little today. Resting and watching Christmas movies will sort it out and then I'll be fine, as I've said before, I am learning to listen to my body and if resting is what I need, then that's what I'll do. I will be okay.

Week 14 Done
23/12/2020

14 weeks finished, and 10 more to do, yesterday was eerily quiet at the hospital, there was only one-half of the treatment side operating with less nurses hurrying around and less people coming and going. I was in and out in 25 minutes and that included a chat with my nurse.

This last week, I have mostly slept and rested, I did feel much better yesterday, my back wasn't as sore and I felt more normal. For some reason, last night, I didn't sleep at all and am feeling it now. I'm very grumpy (sorry hubby) and think I will be sleeping for a while this afternoon.

I watched Bambi II during the night, and I wasn't impressed, why do they have to mess around with the Disney classics, why could they not leave them? It's probably just a money-making exercise, but it did help pass some time.

I can't believe Christmas Day is a few days away, certainly doesn't feel very Christmassy, just very strange and surreal. Add to the mix, the ever-changing what we can or can't do and it's certainly going to be different this year. Whatever it is, and, however, it's celebrated. I hope everybody has a good day and I wish you all, a safe and Happy Christmas.

Still appreciating, the ongoing love and support from everyone. It's what keeps me smiling, focused and staying positive and the knowledge, at some point next year, I will be able to meet up with people again and have those so much-needed hugs.

This week, my chat is short and sweet, my brain through tiredness is not functioning very well and the number of mistakes I'm having to correct is ridiculous. I apologise if I've not sorted all of them and some of this doesn't quite make sense. I am much better this week, I am good. Be kind to yourself and to each other, none of us truly knows what other people are going through in these strange times.

Week 15 Done
30/12/2020

15 weeks done, 9 more to go and I'm quite excited to be in single figures, 9 weeks left to go of my treatment, not sure, if excited is the correct terminology, but for me, the end of treatment is very much in my sights.

I had a lovely Christmas Day with hubby, my daughters and grandkids and thanks to my eldest for doing most of the cooking. My energy levels are definitely lower in this half of my treatment as I spent most of Sunday snoozing and chilling out and, of course, going back into lockdown there isn't much else to do anyway.

I've had notifications due to my vulnerability that I shouldn't go out unless it is to exercise, Zoom calls and WhatsApp chats it is then. My eldest was working in the ICU yesterday with COVID-19 patients, it really brings it home how bad it is at the moment and she really emphasised about me not going anywhere near any shops.

My youngest has been getting the shopping for us and I have a home delivery slot booked for Monday, so that'll keep us going, especially, as she's now gone back to uni to catch up on some work.

Apart from tiredness, my knee has actually not been too painful this last week, no constipation, my back has been sore to the point that paracetamol isn't always strong enough, so when I speak to Dr Noel, I'm going to see if I can get some stronger painkillers.

Last night, I actually slept more than I was awake, what a result. So, I feel quite rested and will probably take myself for a little walk in a bit. Still have my moustache/bristly chin issues, which the face masks hide quite nicely and hubby hasn't mentioned it anymore so I'm guessing he's just got used to it.

I did notice how much longer the hairs on my arms seem to be, that's a bit scary, especially as my hair is supposed to be thinning, it's like I have gorilla arms, but only as far as my elbows! But then, nobody gets to see them except hubby and seeing as I pointed it out to him, he can't say anything, he just agrees with me.

When I write my blog I notice, when I'm tired or struggling I come across as a bit negative, I don't mean to be, but seeing as the point of writing this is to tell it exactly as I feel it and sometimes, I just feel like crap. It is a tough journey and different for every single person, no matter what type of cancer is being fought.

Cancer isn't nice, it isn't kind, it is hard not only on the person fighting it but on family and friends. I am a positive person, I will put this myeloma into remission and I will get to have many more years to do what I want with my family and friends. I know I'll be living with it. It'll never quite go away and at this moment, I have no idea if it will restrict me in any way.

I'll just deal with that when the time comes. Life is too short anyway, and I intend to make the most of whatever my normal will be, enjoying life with my family and friends. Hopefully, by the time I've finished my treatment, I'll be able to see everyone whenever I want and wherever I want.

Today is a good day, I am good.

Christmas and New Year are done and dusted, it was quite low-key but lovely to have the family around. As it was the holidays we still had no date for our move, Pete could no longer help pack, carry stuff or clean, he could, however, get rid of the furniture that was going to be too big for our new home.

I was left to do the packing and cleaning. I had to do it, and couldn't leave a house without cleaning it (this included wiping inside of window frames, and skirting boards and wiping walls down) which at times caused me so much pain, resulting in tears and Pete having to put a pain patch on my back for me.

"Why do you do it," Pete asks, "no one will care."

But I care, I need to know I'll be leaving a clean house, even if the house we're moving to isn't clean. I will have peace of mind, no matter how much pain it'll cause me.

Pete's mobility was starting to slow down, I hated going upstairs behind him, it frightened the life out of me. It's been a while since his diagnosis but as yet, no support from anyone. It was so scary, not knowing how to help or what to do for him.

Pete has started looking at different forms of mobility scooters to help keep his independence, a portable one, so it can be folded into the back of our car and a bigger either three or four-wheeled one, so he can take himself out and about.

Week 16 Done
06/01/2021

16 weeks done, 8 more to go, I'm two-thirds of the way through, and yesterday started cycle five of my treatment, one more infusion to go, yippee. Yesterday, was a late one, treatment was at 5:30 pm, really don't like going that late especially on infusion days as I have to wait for my months' worth of medication.

This means, that by the time I got home, it was well after 7 pm before I took it and then taking everything again this morning (could have taken meds later but need to keep to my routine, or else I'll probably forget to take them) means almost a double dose of steroids. All I'm hoping is hubby doesn't suffer too badly at the end of the week!

When I had the infusion it was really weird yesterday, I could literally feel the stuff going up around my shoulders, couldn't feel it anywhere else just there. Last week, I slept a lot. I'm assuming the chemo is taking its toll on me this half of my treatment my back is definitely sorer (hubby does a lovely gentle back rub that really helps ease it), my knee is easier.

I still have constipation issues, Movicol definitely helps and I control how much I need, as I've learnt, too much of it can send me running for the toilet. My hair seems to be falling out even more, or it could just be my imagination, but I don't think so.

This week the steroids have left me very puffy, swollen or just fat, *mainly on my face (I've looked a bit like a chipmunk some days) and a couple of very bitchy days for hubby, my stomach is always big. Some days, it's bigger than others, hence the range of underwear and sadly big girl pants are the norm most days but it's a small price to pay and hopefully, a temporary one.*

Last night, I was asleep out for the count just after 10 pm and woke up to go to the toilet. I thought it was just after 1 pm, great for me; three solid hours of sleep, nope, it was just after 12, still, that was two hours of sleep. I managed to doze for a while and finally, went downstairs just before 2 am.

I finished listening to my book, put on the film 'Lazy Susan', and snuggled down on the sofa, at which point my back, especially around my shoulder blades became uncomfortable. It was a strange pain, a constant dull ache, after much shuffling around, I found a comfortable position and at some point fell asleep.

I missed the later part of the film, so, will catch up with it later. I still feel shattered, but for me, napping quite a lot through the night is good. I'll take myself for a little walk in between the showers and then have a nap later because I can, and my body obviously needs it (and I have learnt to listen to my body).

So, we're into another lockdown, much needed but still, Boo, not that I was going out anywhere, but when you're told not, it makes you want to go out, but I'm not. Just means, I have to wait even longer for those all-important hugs.

The first thought that popped into my head was, "Bugger, I can't get my haircut."

I'd made the decision to go short, to help me get used to the idea of having no hair. My youngest completed her Brave the Shave challenge by shaving her hair off (helped by her sister) and has raised £2000 so far for Macmillan Cancer, I am so very proud of her and her achievement.

Thank you to everyone who has donated. It's not too late for anyone wanting to donate and also for your words of support, we really appreciate it. She did say, it felt very strange, but is getting used to it, which sealed my thoughts on trying to prepare for my hair falling out, hence, me wanting a short haircut.

Had some great news, it wasn't Dr Noel but whoever she was, told me I had no infection in my blood whatsoever. Fantastic, the medication has definitely done its job and so makes what I'm going through worthwhile.

Be kind to yourselves and talk to each other, I am very good.

Lots have been going on over the last week or so, a visit from the therapy team at St Micheal's Hospice, we have a perch stool so Pete can sit and still cook, or make a drink and one upstairs so Pete can wash and shave without fear of falling over.

A stair lift was suggested, no point in this house, as it would be a waste of money, a riser recliner chair and various other things to help make life easier for Pete and grants that were available to help buy these things. A referral to wheelchair services, to see about an electric wheelchair.

I didn't see the point of having a manual one as I wouldn't be able to push Pete without doing myself damage. Most of this was to be put in place when we moved, so, as soon as we have an actual date, we needed to let them know, and then appointments for Pete could be booked in.

It was so nice and reassuring to have support and people knowing what Pete needed, we were also given a number for an MND visitor, who would normally come out to visit us, but due to COVID restrictions, it was phone calls or Zoom calls only.

I didn't like doing Zoom calls, so was quite happy to phone and chat. Pete didn't want anything to do with it, which was fine, at least, I could ask questions and get answers to things that were constantly going around in my head.

Week 17 Done
13/01/2021

17 done, 7 more to go. It was quieter at the hospital and I was in and out within half an hour, very good and very efficient. My injection does seem to hurt or smart *more as the weeks have gone on, is it my stomach area protesting or different nurses inject it differently to cause discomfort, who knows.*

Lots of pain, discomfort and tears over the last week due to the infusion. I did enquiry about stronger pain killers but it seems they can cause constipation, so I've decided the achy pain is better to deal with than the constipation issue seeing as I've only just got on top of constipation and the pain it caused, is far worse than my aching/sore body.

This meant, I have spent the best part of the week sleeping and resting and taking myself out for the odd walk, which I must say, is certainly helping my knee and helping my breathlessness. I have to make sure, I pace myself or I return home puffing away like a steam train.

My hair seems to be constantly dropping out, not in handfuls but in strands, it might be my imagination and the fact the hoover seems to contain a lot of my hair when I empty it (which is quite regularly).

Sadly, my gorilla-like arms don't seem to be reducing nor does the facial moustache/beard area. Thankfully, with lockdown no one sees me (except hubby and he hasn't dared mention it since last time) and hopefully, it will have disappeared by the time we're actually able to see other people again.

Walking as I have said, seems to have eased my knees and breathlessness, my face felt so fat last weekend I could almost feel my eyes closing up (thank you, steroids) and I did think I might have to get even bigger big girl pants (God forbid), guess I could always resort to borrowing hubby's boxer shorts as a last resort.

Thankfully, on Sunday, after spending lots of time weeing, my body size did start to reduce, if anyone remembers the advert with the Michelin tyre man, that's what I felt like and I'm sure looked like. I know some of it is my imagination, but when you can literally feel you're body swelling up it's not good.

Supposedly, I need to drink more to wee more to get rid of the fluid retention, which is hard when I don't feel like drinking, feel very sick and don't really want to eat. I can't wait for my very muzzy head to return to some sort of normality either, I can't remember things, can't concentrate, if you could see what I was typing.

I'm gobsmacked at myself, thank goodness for spell check to correct my very many mistakes, I'm even sitting here, not able to spell words I know how to spell, or trying to think of a word I want to use, it's ridiculous and very surreal.

The side effects, which seem to be hitting me harder as my treatment progresses, which I guess is to be expected, are more uncomfortable and restricting than anything, but I can do this, putting up with the discomfort short-term far outweighs the long-term benefits.

I miss seeing my family, and I miss seeing my friends (I should have been going to the Isle of Wight on Friday for the weekend with an amazing bunch of ladies. Sadly, it is postponed until next year.).

I miss hugs so much and social interaction, I know everyone is in the same situation on this front, but it just makes a rubbish situation a lot harder, so thank you for your continued support and messages, it means so much and really helps keep me going, especially, on my not-so-good days.

Life is hard for everyone at the moment, look out for each other and be kind to each other. I am good.

Week 18 Done
20/01/2021

18 weeks done, 6 more to do. I'm three-quarters of the way through my treatment and the end is in sight. Even though the hospital appeared quiet yesterday for my 4:30 pm appointment, I still waited until almost 5 pm before I was called through, and then I was in, jab done and out again in less than five minutes.

I just don't like going late in the afternoon for my appointments, a real positive was the fact it was still light when I arrived, shame it was practically pitch black when I came out, another few weeks and it'll still be light, does make a difference, to me anyway.

So how have I been this last week? Tired, but not sleeping as much, my energy levels are definitely reduced, and my back is still sore (the long hot water bottle is a real godsend as it reaches the length of my spine, and then I flip it across both my shoulders, creating some relief).

My nurse suggested possibly trying some sort of pain relief patch, she was going to discuss it with Dr Noel and get him to prescribe it, if it was acceptable for me to have, there was nothing to pick up when I had my jab yesterday. So, I'll chase the outcome with her later.

My head is slightly more lucid today, but that doesn't mean I won't make mistakes or forget what I was trying to say. That is one of the things I find really frustrating. I'm asked something, or if I've put something somewhere, my face is blank.

I honestly can't remember, still can't read a book or watch anything too complicated on TV, audiobooks seem to work for me and I can usually manage a few chapters before I lose concentration or nod off. My knee continues to cause me some pain but I am so much more mobile, so that's acceptable.

The scary thing that seems to be happening on a Saturday is my face swells up, a few weeks back, I thought I was having a reaction to the cat, itchy eyes, itchy body, and puffy face and took antihistamines (then found out I shouldn't take them, oops).

My face swelled again the following Saturday causing red, sore eyes and this Saturday hubby actually watched my face swell up like a puffer fish and my eye reduced to almost slits, it's obliviously a reaction to one or more of the medication I'm on. I asked the nurse giving me my jab if it was anything I should worry about, and she said it was best to ask my nurse, so I will.

A few months ago, hubby was diagnosed with motor neurone disease, not something we were obviously expecting and sadly meant having to have another conversation with our kids and tell them, never an easy thing to tell those you love, family or friends. I am so proud of the kids, how they have coped and dealt with the news in their different ways, obviously, it is still sinking in.

For me, there have been many tears and there will be many more, it is another challenge in life, one we will adjust to together and deal with as a family, it may take a while, but life is too short, and we need to enjoy it (bit hard at the moment, but it will get better).

Live life and love life, today, I am good.

It's been a busy few weeks, finally, a move date set and the removal company booked, we move on Wednesday, 2 March, not a great choice of days as I have treatment in Winchester at 5 pm, but we'll sort it one way or the other.

Pete has had another specialist appointment, not great news as the MND he has, is the faster-acting one, we can't do anything about it, so let's face it and deal with it.

There are a few trials going on that Pete may be able to get on, so we'll apply for those, anything that will help make life easier and hopefully prolong it, will be good. Pete has a set of sitting yoga sessions via Zoom booked to help keep him as mobile and supple as possible.

He has also been prescribed Riluzole, which may help him by possibly 10% it may not, but anything is worth a try. I just cannot believe there is nothing to help MND sufferers. To stop the progression of the disease and help prolong their lives, just nothing at all, very scary and sad.

I know there are different types of MND, some more life-limiting than others and the way the disease affects people is different in each individual. I haven't read much about the disease as I don't want to know at the moment what we are facing.

We just need to take it one day at a time, enjoy life and make memories. 10 years ago, my cancer would have been more of a death sentence for me, but thanks to research and ongoing improvements in treatments, life expectancy is looking much better and brighter as is the quality of life. Sad, the same cannot be said for MND sufferers.

Wheelchair services have also been out to visit Pete with a view to getting him an electric wheelchair, there is no point doing anything at the moment, and we need to let them know as soon as we've moved.

Week 19 Done
27/01/2021

19 done, 5 more to go, my appointment was at 12:30 pm yesterday, and I was back in the car by 12:40 pm, what a result. I was told that I would now need a weekly COVID test, obviously getting a negative result before I could have my treatment and any future blood tests were to be carried out in the same place, a building opposite St Michaels Hospice, for Haemophilia patients, which means, I don't enter the main hospital at all.

In this present climate, which suits me, anything to keep myself safer. Unfortunately, the pain relief patch still wasn't at Sarum Road for me to pick up. Victoria my nurse was already on it and I received an email from her as I sat down to be called through for my treatment telling me.

I did manage to talk to her as I was leaving and again asked about my stem cell stuff as I've still not heard anything. She was able to tell me they are still harvesting bone marrow, so doesn't know why I've still not heard anything and will chase it. Within half an hour of getting home from my treatment, I had a call from Basingstoke pharmacy apologising for not sending my meds. Did I want to go pick them up? Obviously not, they have been posted and should arrive tomorrow. Sorted.

I thought I had the measure of the effects of my medication, but it seems not, it still throws me out and does exactly what it wants. Last Thursday, hubby couldn't say a word to me without me either growling or snapping at him, the sad thing is I know I'm doing it but can't stop myself.

Sorry hubby, sadly, I doubt if it'll be the last time either. Friday was spent either sleeping or crying. Saturday I was again like a puffed-up fish. (if anyone has seen the film 'Shallow Hal', that's how I feel, maybe, not quite as big)

Thankfully, I've not had to resort to buying even bigger big girl pants, but there is still time, it's a small price to pay for getting me better and most of it should disappear when I finish my medication (fingers crossed).

My hair is still dropping out, my beard, and moustache and now it seems nose hair is still causing me concern, to the point I think I'm going to have to resort to trimming my nose hair with hubby's trimmer (if Iwork out how to use it).

It could be my hair has lightened (no not grey) considerably during treatment, making it more noticeable to me, let's face it, I don't have a lot to do with my time at the moment, so noticing these things is bound to happen.

Constipation was a bit of an issue (nothing like before), just a little uncomfortable, sorted with the help of Movicol. I've been okay for a while, so it was a bit of a pain in more ways than one. My back, neck and shoulders were sore for a few days (yes, could have done with the patch), hot water bottle, paracetamol and back rub from hubby helped ease it and I'm glad to say, at the moment I'm pain-free.

I've slept a lot (apart from last night being awake since 12:30 getting up at 2 am, falling asleep at 5:30 am, and woken up by the cat at 7:15 am), watched both Marcella's. I'm so glad it's back, love this programme, and caught up with other TV. I'm sure, I'll be having a nap later, maybe, after a little walk, if it stops raining.

For all the rubbish going on with my body, I'm actually feeling good in myself. I'm happy, finding things to laugh about, and chatting to family and friends, whose ongoing support is such a blessing and boost.

Like everyone, still miss actually seeing people and not being able to hug or touch, obviously keeping safe is my top priority so I'll continue to do what I'm doing for as long as it takes.

Stay safe everyone, look out for each other, share the love and laugh.

I am good.

Packing is going really well, a lot of our bigger furniture has either been sold or rehomed, yes I still struggle to do what I shouldn't be doing (mainly scrubbing the house), but then I wouldn't be me if I didn't.

Pete's mobility is more noticeable, we have had the car adapted with hand controls, so Pete is still able to drive. He does find the steering really heavy on this car for some reason, so we are getting it checked out, just in case, there is something wrong.

Pete is now the proud owner of a little portable mobility scooter that sits in the boot of the car (even though it is light, I still struggle to get it in/out of the boot and sadly, Pete can't help for fear of him falling over, but I'll do it regardless) and a bigger mobility scooter that he can take himself out and about on.

The first one arrived and hadn't been set up for Pete to control it with his left hand, he can't do much at all with his right, so there is no point even taking delivery of it. Seeing as it's going back, Pete has decided to change his mind about the four-wheeled version and go for a three-wheeler instead. I don't think there is much difference in the price, so he may as well go with what he wants.

Week 20 Done
03/02/2021

Week 20 is done, 4 more weeks to go, five cycles completed, and the sixth and final cycle started yesterday, it really doesn't seem like any time at all since I posted my first post all those weeks ago, probably because in my brain fog of pills I spend quite a lot of time napping and time passes quite quickly, which I'm glad about.

Yesterday, after my infusion and injection, for the first time since starting the treatment, I actually felt like poo when I got home, light head, generally feeling yukky and totally exhausted (thankfully hubby and I had already agreed to have a takeout for tea).

The only thing different was I had my first COVID injection on Monday (thankfully with no side effects). I'd just fallen asleep when the house phone rang (it was usually Dr or hospital, so felt it had to be answered), there's nothing worse than trying to talk to someone when you're not really with it (guess it might be what it's like if I drank and was drunk).

I couldn't answer the lady's questions and couldn't even open emails on my phone, had to switch to the iPad, goodness knows what she must have thought. It was a nurse from the

Rainbow unit, there was a hiccup with my medication that I didn't find out about until I got home. So, I messaged Victoria to see who I needed to talk to, she had got in touch with the Rainbow unit hence the phone call.

I've had a call from the pharmacy this morning, so all is hopefully, now sorted. Tiredness is defiantly more noticeable these days, but then Iam able to nap when I want, so it is not too much of an issue. I have to remind myself considering the amount of chemo and other drugs now in my body, that it is okay to not be okay, there is bound to be ongoing fallout from it.

I have used the pain relief patches, which do help, I'm only using them when I really need to. For some reason, my knee has been particularly sore this last week. I'm still able to walk (hobble) and bend it which is a great improvement from the first few months when I couldn't even walk on it and for some reason, constipation is causing not major problems but a few issues, Movicol as always is helping.

Still, need to up my fluid intake (do wonder if I did drink wine, would it eliminate this issue and no, I'm not about to try it out), which would probably help with constipation and fluid retention. Yes, I'm still puffing up but thankfully not quite as much (helped I think by taking antihistamines).

My mood swings are awful, poor hubby, as you can guess I'm still snapping or biting his head off, for next to no reason, hopefully, not for much longer (goodness knows what excuse I can use when I'm off my medication).

I had my monthly call from Dr Noel, blood is still completely clear, in his eyes putting me in remission, he is so pleased and has been chasing Southampton about my stem cell harvesting, so much so, that I have a phone consultation on 16 February with the consultant from Southampton.

Hopefully, this will enlighten me as to what is going to happen and when, for at least my harvesting. I'm not holding out for a stem cell transplant date due to what's going on with the virus, but it would be nice to know if I have to wait.

I'm guessing, that if I have to wait, I may have to continue with some of the medication, the bone-strengthening infusion was mentioned by Dr Noel, we'll know more by the time I talk to him towards the end of the month and he'll make the decision about what will be best for me.

I had my first virus swab done by a nurse on Saturday, oh my goodness, the throat was no issue (I remember when I did the swab myself, I cried with laughter at the amount of gagging I did and then couldn't do it as I was laughing so much), it was the nose bit, It felt like she was trying to reach my brain or some such place too far up, to surely be still part of my nose.

My nose was smarting for the rest of the day and I have the joys of this to look forward to every Saturday as long as I'm going to Sarum Road. Good to know, the test was negative and if it was positive where would I have picked it up from, haven't seen anyone or been out apart from walking, but it wasn't so all is good.

Thank you to everyone for your continued support, love and messages, hopefully, as my treatment comes to an end, we may have an easing of the lockdown to actually be able to see people socially distanced and in the not-too-distant future hug people. I really can't wait for that day.

Be kind, stay positive and laugh. I am good.

Pete became the proud owner of a mobility scooter, which is adapted to be used by his left hand and gives him more freedom and independence, his idea is to be able to join the ladies from his running club (we have given them the name of Pete's harem), bringing a bit of normality into a life that so isn't normal.

Pete has also had a couple of interviews regarding trials to do with MND, fingers crossed; hope he gets accepted in, or at least on one of them.

Week 21 Done
10/02/2021

21 weeks done, 3 more to go, so, can't wait to finish all the medication, or have less anyway. Reading up on what'll happen before my bone marrow harvesting, I'll need more injections and obviously, when I go into hospital for my transplant, I'll be on medication most of which will be given intravenously.

It has freaked me out a little reading about what'll happen, it'll all sink in and I'll be fine, the only thing that really bothers me is my hair falling out and I don't know why. It's not a vanity thing, I think it might make me feel a bit vulnerable. I have chemo hair hats to wear, so no one would really know any different outside of the house.

I'm sure, I'll be fine when it actually happens. Last week, I slept and slept, my bones were achy, not too sore and I only needed paracetamol to help with the discomfort. Due to the meds cocked up, I did feel really sick for most of the week and for a change had a bit of an upset stomach rather than constipation.

(All meds were sorted yesterday, so all should be fine this week.)

Very emotional at the weekend and again for some reason yesterday after my chemo. We had an Iceland delivery due, they delivered only four items, no sweets, biscuits or cake amongst other things. I almost cried because I really wanted some sweets, the poor delivery man checked his van but no, the rest of my order wasn't there.

Hubby phoned them up and fair play to them and the lovely delivery man, he dropped most of the order around to me a few hours later. Yes, some things were still missing and should have been delivered today, but I got the all-important sweets.

Why on earth did a food delivery make me upset, to the point of coming inside and actually sobbing and spending the next few hours crying on and off is beyond me.

Obviously not beyond my fragile mind and I should remember I am totally unpredictable when it comes to my emotional state; a song can reduce me to tears, something on the TV, a look or comment from hubby or I can become totally unreasonable, snappy and crabby, still it meant lots of cuddles with hubby and much appreciated they were.

Definitely more settled this morning even with only two hours of sleep, I was downstairs, finally falling asleep around 5:45 am, can't even remember what film I watched. Definitely having a sleep later. Been out for a few walks, not in the icy, snowy conditions, didn't fancy slipping over and having a trip to A&E, no broken/chipped bones for me thank you very much.

My head is still a fuzzy mess most of the time and my ability to remember (as with the film I watched earlier) is rubbish. Sending messages is very much a hit-and-miss, so apologies if you receive something and you think what on

Earth is she on. I do try to sort them out before sending, but not always before I've pressed the send button.

I am really enjoying my virtual shopping trips with Liv, she takes me to her food shop, and we walk to the shop, discussing what she needs and what she's going to cook with it as we walk around. It's the nearest I've been food shopping for what seems like months.

We were in Lidl the other day, she got all this food, I asked her how much it had cost £37, a bargain. We then walk back and chat as she puts the food away or if she makes too much noise I leave her to it, thanks Liv for helping me get out, even if it is virtually.

I can't wait to be able to do something other than watch TV and I watch a lot, listening to my audible books can only be done for a while as my mind will start wandering or I'll snooze and miss a chunk of the story and have to go back, even colouring can only be done in small bursts and to read an actual book, definitely not doable at the moment.

Today is a good day, I'm sitting typing, looking out of the window on a lovely very cold, sunny day with the ice melting, a red kite flying low over the trees and a squirrel running around in the garden.

Be good to each other, be kind to each other and stay safe. I am happy. I am good.

Week 22 Done
17/02/2021

22 weeks done 2 more to go. I am just so excited, only one more chemo jab. I just can't wait for my body to start returning to some sort of normality. In the world we're living in, who knows what normal is anyway? Yesterday, my treatment appointment for the first time was earlier, from having my temperature taken, checks done and jabbed I was in and out within 20 minutes, what a result.

I definitely need to nap more this last month of my treatment and am more tired, if that is the only full-out from the amount of treatment I've had, I can deal with that. Obviously, all the other smaller ongoing issues are still around but it is all cope-able.

Puffing up, especially at the weekend, I am steadily putting on a little bit of weight each week, regardless of what I have or haven't eaten, or how much I poo or don't poo (it does amaze me on the rare occasion throughout my treatment I go to the toilet a lot that I never lose weight, why is that?).

My knee is still sore, my hair is dropping out, my chin is stubble, my moustache and nose hairs still have a growing rate of their own and the hairs on my arms. Well, I was feeling a little chilly the other day and my arm hairs (not under the arm) seemed to have doubled in quantity, I'm sure I could have almost plaited them, they just needed sadly to be a little longer.

Some days, I feel really sick, mainly towards the end of the week, some days, I'm an emotional wreck, this is never predictable and I will cry at the slightest thing or cry at nothing, usually, Thursdays are my crabby, snappy days, it can last longer, especially if I've not slept much.

My sleeping is up and down. Tuesdays seem to be the one constant of not sleeping, it was around 5 am before I finally dropped off this morning, two and a half hours of sleep and I've not slept very well for a couple of nights before, so I am starting to feel a little jaded.

It's not like I have much to do anyway, so I just nap as and when I need to or have a lay-in. Like so, many people at the moment, I do struggle with feeling very isolated, not being able to go out apart from a walk (weather permitting), missing those so important hugs and speaking to people face to face. I know hubby is with me which is great but even we need a break from each other, now and again.

My COVID tests are getting easier, my nose thankfully hasn't been as sore as it was the first week and there was no blood last week, the nurse did say I was one of the easiest people to test, that's because I've learnt to relax myself as I found it didn't hurt as much.

I got a call from the consultant at Southampton yesterday, my bone marrow harvesting is at the end of March, and blood tests and injections beforehand (injections to stimulate more bone marrow), so that's really positive.

No date for a transplant apart from probably May/June time, COVID has delayed everything so I just have to be patient. The consultant was really nice and did warn me; that I would feel very ill, sick, with diarrhoea, mouth sores, and tiredness.

I would be in hospital for two to three weeks, where I should be feeling my worst, even when I've been given my healthy bone marrow I will feel extremely tired for the first few weeks and will need support when I come out of hospital.

It will take a while for me to get some immunity back, so I will be very vulnerable. I did ask about the COVID-jab as I will be getting my second dose next week, will I still keep some protection? It's obviously not a question he could answer as it's an unknown, they'll test to see if I have antibodies in my system and go from there.

Should I be allowed another jab if there are none in my system, I would have already had my two, guess that's something to think about when I have my transplant. It is all very positive.

The weather is certainly warmer this week, unfortunately with it comes the grey wet dreariness. I think I'd rather prefer the cold with bright sunny skies, sadly, it's not something anyone has any control over, blue skies and sunshine definitely make me feel better even if I am freezing.

Why do I talk about the weather, I'm sitting overlooking my garden typing, listening to the wind, watching the trees blowing and the first buds appearing on them and the rain falling.

Apart from tiredness, I am good, I am excited as I near the end of my treatment cycle. I have so much to be thankful for, the ongoing love and support from my family and friends, without whom I would've struggled to get through these last few months. Life throws us these curve balls, it's how you throw them back, that counts.

Be safe, be kind, be happy. I'm good.

Just about everything that isn't coming with us has been sold, given away or binned, more or less everything has been packed up and most of the cleaning has been done.

I've so missed Pete's help with the manual stuff and my body has suffered, who knew a cocktail of medication could affect your body and life so much? I am exhausted, not just with my treatment but with the whole packing up house moving process and there are a lot of things Pete can no longer do, which is scary in itself.

Thankfully, Pete is able to do all the paperwork and admin stuff (don't think my brain could cope at the moment with any form of paperwork).

Week 23 Done
24/02/2021

23 weeks done, 1 more to go, to say I'm excited to be on my final week is an understatement. I had my final chemo jab yesterday, a week of other medication then my body can rest and I'll hopefully get my headspace back. (Yesterday, I was almost incapable of stringing a sentence together and couldn't remember who my car insurer was.)

Tiredness is definitely the main issue for me at the moment, I nap when I need to and surprisingly last night, I had a good five hours of sleep, the best ever Tuesday night since I started my treatment.

Constipation has reared its ugly head, nowhere near as bad as the first time, but enough to make me uncomfortable whilst carefully taking Movicol, all is back to normal now, let's hope it stays that way. My back has been sore and I had to put a pain relief patch on over the weekend, they most definitely helped and gave me a good night's sleep which is always a bonus.

My body seems to have been constantly bloated this past week and my face is most definitely fat (I don't like using that word makes me worry this excess weight won't come off, it'll be what it'll be and considering what has been in my body I shouldn't beat myself up about it).

Loads of my hair seem to be dropping out, the hoover has to be constantly emptied but it only really shows on the top of my head, which I don't think most people would even notice. A headband or scarf disguises it quite nicely if I really want to cover it up.

Shame my bristly bits aren't given the same treatment, there is the thought they may not even be related to my treatment but to my age, not a thought I really want to consider at the moment.

Emotions are still all over the place, definitely more tearful at any given day or time, with no reasoning behind it. I now just go with the flow and again with my little temper outbursts, let it go, hubby usually gets it in the neck, and even though he's used to them it's still not nice.

The trouble is I won't have any excuse when the meds have worked their way out of my system, that's something I'll have to think about.

It'll be so nice to be able to read a book again. I finally finished my second audiobook on Monday, four months of listening to two books, is not bad, at least, it gives me something to do when I can't sleep at night. It's strange, I can never settle to listen to them during the day for some reason, maybe, I'll be able to as my head settles down.

I am tired but very happy and excited, I know I've still got a lot to deal with moving forward but I'll cope with whatever. I'm looking forward to my chat with Dr Noel later in the week to see what he has in store for me outside my treatment cycle.

No more hospital visits (for a while hopefully) should mean no more COVID tests, although I must say it was a younger nurse doing the testing this week and it didn't hurt at all, she was much gentler, or maybe, I've got used to them and am more relaxed anyway.

Stay safe, be kind to yourself and others, Live life, love life and laugh. I am good.

After having got the car checked for steering issues and nothing found we decided to look for an easier car for Pete to drive, we are now the proud owners of a Mercedes GLC, hand controls were installed before we picked it up, so Pete was able to drive it away from the garage and so much easier for him to handle.

Anything that keeps Pete mobile and helps his independence is a given at this moment in our lives.

Week 24 Done
03/03/2021

24 weeks of my first treatment cycle was completed. This included 6 x bone-strengthening infusions 24 x chemo jabs 168 x blood thinning jabs (given by myself), 168 x thalidomide pills, 48 x days of steroids plus antibiotics, Movicol, painkillers and other medication.

For the time being, I'm having the bone-strengthening infusion, antibiotics, gout pills and calcium and vitamin D. I'm more than happy with that.

So, in the last week of treatment, I'm still tired, still having issues around constipation, and my knee is still sore especially if I bend down too much. I actually slept better on Tuesday for the first time since starting the treatment (no steroids or chemo), my face is still fat/bloated, my belly is still big and yes I still have to wear my big girl pants.

I made hubby feel my bristly chin the other day, and he wasn't amused, my hair is still dropping out, my nails have been splitting and my back is very sore. I nap when I need to and my head is still all over the place. Fingers crossed over the next few weeks, the majority of these will calm down.

I can't wait to start driving again. It's been almost six months or so of not being able to hold a conversation without having to search my brain for the right words if I can even remember why I wanted that word when I finally find it or actually remember a conversation.

Why am I so late writing my blog? Tuesday after almost six months, we finally moved house and also I hadn't realised I still had to continue with my infusion, so I had to go to Winchester for treatment. It was a bit of a manic day.

Monday, I thought it would take a couple of hours to finish sorting what needed doing. At 8 pm, exhausted, in pain and an emotional wreck, I finally finished, and help was offered, in my mind I could cope, well I couldn't and I suffered for my stubbornness, lesson learnt, accept offers of help, what I think I can do, I can't.

All the stress associated with house moving has finally gone, and my medication has reduced considerably. I've had my second COVID jab, and spring is in the air, so much to look forward to.

Be happy, be safe, I am good.

We have finally moved; we used a removal company and Cheryl took a big part as she actually oversaw the move. When I got home after treatment, the bed was already made, neither Pete nor I had to do very much (not that either of us had the energy) and lots of boxes had been unpacked.

You know when you have good friends and appreciate them so much, our new furniture was delivered before the carpet was laid in the living room, the furniture was moved around for us and then unboxed and put together. We now have a living room where we can sit and relax. It didn't take Pete long to familiarise himself with the reclining chair!

It is also quite apparent that downsizing, even after a massive clear-out, we're still struggling to find somewhere for everything to go, especially in the kitchen, so Pete is going to re-jig the kitchen (it is his job to design them so he'll know exactly what to do).

We have a five-ring gas burner that I don't want and it is unsafe for Pete, so we'll have a smaller, safer, induction hob installed, an oven with a sliding door and if I'm lucky, we'll get a bit more cupboard space squeezed in.

If the understairs cupboard is shelved out, I'll be able to sort it. If nothing else, it gives Pete something to focus on, it's his area of expertise. I've said what I want and I'll leave it to him.

Our kids and our friends really stepped up to help us settle in, doing things that ordinarily we would have been able to do ourselves, very frustrating for us and also very humbling, but we are in our new home and now, we can get the ball rolling for the things Pete needs to make his life easier and safer.

Chemo Cycle Finished
10/03/2021

So, my chemo cycle has finished, but that doesn't mean I've finished my blog. I've still a long way to go and lots to share. I've been taken off a lot of my meds and my body is all over the place but I feel more like me, strange as it may seem.

I have more energy some days, and my head is clearer but my brain is not computing as I would like at the moment, hopefully, normality will return in the not-too-distant future. My emotions are all over the place, my face is no longer a puffer fish and is slowly returning to a more normal look, and my stomach is slowly deflating but sadly I'm still wearing big girl pants.

Am I expecting too much of my body in such a short time, of course, I am, guess I just want to be normal for a while before my stem cell transplant. As I was told in my initial diagnosis, my myeloma is treatable, not curable, the treatment will give me the chance to lead as normal a life (whatever normal is these days) as possible.

Last Tuesday, we moved house, we've been waiting to move, mostly packed up since before Christmas, always being told we were waiting for one more issue to be resolved, I have never felt so frustrated.

One week on, with the help of some wonderful, supportive people, we have a bit of normality in our home, a comfy living room, a table we can eat off of, yes, still boxes to be opened, things to find homes for but we are getting there.

The relief and lightness I felt as all the pressure from moving house finally went away is unimaginable. We sold our house around the time of my diagnosis, initially, when our house was put on the market last March, the idea was to sell up, downsize and move to be nearer the sea as our youngest went off to uni, pay off a chunk of our mortgage and free up some money with which to enjoy ourselves.

It was made very clear that now was not a time to be moving away, so we didn't and found this house just after I started my treatment, it took the best part of six months to complete and be where we now are.

Now, I can concentrate on myself and my hubby, there is still lots going on, but life is an adventure, sometimes that adventure is not of our choosing, but how we choose to cope or deal with it is.

Be happy, be safe. I am good.

All through my treatment, I have had to have numerous blood tests and before every treatment a COVID test, my arm feels like a pin cushion and I don't think my nose will ever be the same again, it has to be what it has to be.

I'm due another bone marrow test in anticipation of my bone marrow being harvested (fingers crossed). I'm still reliant on being driven around as my head has not cleared enough for me to want to drive (I've not been told not to drive, it's entirely my choice), thankfully, Pete is still driving (just about).

We've also had a stair lift installed, I can breathe when Pete goes upstairs, no more fear of him falling down them, we were advised to rent the stair lift rather than buy it, didn't want to ask any questions about the reasoning behind it, an answer I don't want to hear!

Happy
24/03/2021

After an initial burst of energy and thinking, I felt more normal, last week my energy bubble burst and I literally had no energy. I also felt constantly sick, my body itched, my left knee was so sore and the amount of hair dropping out of my head was unbelievable, I'm surprised I'm not bald.

I was having a shower, it was the worst shower ever, I washed my hair (big mistake) the more I tried to wash, the more hair seemed to attach itself to my body, there's nothing worse than not feeling clean after a shower. I was literally crying tears of frustration.

My hair is now constantly tied up so it doesn't drop into everything I do. Guess it's the comedown from all the meds I was on, hopefully, things should start to settle down soon. I am sleeping better and my head is less fuzzy. I still don't remember much, but that could have to do with my age rather than what I'm going through.

I still don't have a transplant date, but I have been to Southampton for blood tests in preparation for my bone marrow harvesting. I've also had blood taken to check everything is still under control and I've had a bone marrow test to check out how it is after my initial treatment.

I go for my bone marrow harvesting next week. I've been told that it can take up to three days to collect the required amount (which is enough for two transplants) but to expect two days.

I have to inject myself twice a day for four days beforehand to enhance bone marrow growth and I can expect bone pain as a result of these injections, great. I see it as short-term pain for long-term gain.

We have settled into our new home, still lots to do and lots to sort, it's keeping me busy and as long as I'm careful about how much I do, I'm getting things done at my pace and in my time.

Be safe, be kind, be happy. I am good.

A bittersweet day, on one hand, my bone marrow transplant was one step closer, and I started the harvesting of my bone marrow, on the other hand, I left the house having shared a bed with Pete, came home tired and emotional to a hospital bed for Pete and a single two feet six inches bed for me in our bedroom.

(Pete can no longer move himself around in our bed and was finding it increasingly difficult to actually get in or out of the bed)

Very emotional, with many tears after Cheryl had gone and at least thankful Pete couldn't come upstairs to see the mess I was in. There are no words for how I feel, the sadness knowing I'll never share a bed with my man again and bringing home how much his mobility was decreasing.

Again, thanks to Cheryl my bed had been put together and made up, as well as her dropping me at the hospital and picking me up. Hospital transport arriving in the morning to take me for my harvesting as Cheryl will be taking Pete for his respiratory appointment, also at Southampton.

Pete is using a Zimmer frame to get around as he is no longer able to walk unaided, we have one upstairs and one downstairs as I'm not able to bring one up/down the stairs. I did find out that I could climb onto Pete's bed and have a cuddle although it did result in much laughter as I then tried to get back off of the bed.

On a positive note, the garden has been redone, making it wheelchair friendly for Pete, we've opted for astroturf as it'll make it easier for me to maintain and where there was a big step down into the garden there is now a gentle slope.

When Pete's wheelchair arrives, he'll be able to shoot straight out, as he does in his mobility scooter, with access and independence maintained. Now, we need a date for the delivery of the new shed, which will have power installed, so Pete's mobility scooter can be charged and it'll be a dry safe place for it.

Harvesting
01/04/2021

So, the past week has been quite interesting, to say the least, since last Thursday, I've been injecting myself with two injections in the afternoon to help boost my bone marrow production.

As I have been giving myself the blood thinning jab all through my chemo treatment I wasn't fazed by it, which is a good job as the letter telling me I had to do this and what time I had to be at Southampton Hospital on 29 March didn't arrive until 25 March, so if I'd needed a nurse to give me the injections it hadn't left much time to sort it.

Southampton pharmacy phoned to say the injections were on their way, they were with a courier and should be with me just after lunch. I checked they were coming to the right address, and a couple of hours later I got a call to say the courier had gone to my old address and had now left the area so I couldn't have my injections until tomorrow.

I explained I needed to start using them that day, tomorrow would be too late. After numerous phone calls my injections finally turned up, apart from making me feel very sick, they thankfully didn't appear to have any side effects.

My eldest daughter was here early Monday morning and we were at Southampton Hospital just after 8 am. I needed a blood test to check if I would be okay for my harvesting which meant waiting around for an hour, as I'd had my blood done less than a week before, so that I was ready for my monthly call with Dr Noel, those results were all good so it was decided I'd be hooked up to the machine anyway and my daughter wouldn't have to hang around.

Needles in both arms and almost zero mobility as any movement sent alarms off on the machine, even using the phone with my left hand upset the machine, chatting to the staff, listening to the radio or napping was the extent of my activities.

Good harvest on Monday, which was overshadowed by my low potassium count and resulted in a potassium infusion, there's nothing worse than staff leaving to go home whilst I'm still hooked up to a drip for possibly another two and a half hours.

Nurses from another ward were keeping an eye on me and were taking more blood in the hope of getting me home earlier. Three different nurses and four more holes in my hand/arm finally resulted in the required blood and a mini meltdown from me, but blood was not okay, so didn't get to leave the hospital until 6:30 pm.

Back at the hospital, just after 8 am Tuesday morning, I was hooked straight up to the machine, which then proceeded to keep alarming for the first hour. I had to keep both arms very still which finally settled the machine and allowed harvesting to begin.

I was allowed to leave by 2:30 pm, a much better time, even though my potassium levels were still low, I just needed to take the pills given to me the day before.

Just before I got home, my phone rang to say my two days on the machine had harvested more than enough bone marrow for my transplant, the great result was no more days attached to the machine, one very happy me.

I may have bruised hands and arms, ache all over and be very tired, but a few days of chilling and napping will sort me out, another box ticked on my road to recovery, now, I just have to wait for a transplant date.

Be good to each other, be kind to each other and be happy. I am good.

Not so long on the harvesting machine today and what a result I was able to come home with Pete and Cheryl after Pete's respiratory appointment. As Pete's mobility is decreasing it's easier to have friends over, seeing as Pete's birthday is coming up, his mates came to the house.

So lovely to see and hear normality, they don't treat Pete any differently, much alcohol consumed and a slightly merry Pete, I loved it.

I am struggling to help Pete help himself, getting out of bed, dressing, showering, shaving, and going to the toilet, in fact, every day-to-day activity is becoming a challenge.

There are many tears from both of us as I try to help Pete with stuff he wants to be doing for himself and would rather I wasn't doing it for him, especially when it comes to wiping his arse. Not only it is his independence, but it's also Pete's dignity at stake.

Sadly, we need help, I need help. I am really struggling, it upsets me, I can no longer cope with Pete's needs on my own, if I didn't have cancer, maybe, I would be able to do more for him (I'll never know the answer to that).

After a very hard conversation with the therapy team at St Micheal's Hospice, the decision was made to get a care agency involved and a meeting was set up. The initial outcome was for someone to come in every morning to help get Pete up and shower him.

Pete didn't want this, didn't want someone coming into our home doing things that he should be doing for himself, sadly, there was no other choice and it broke my heart, many tears were shed from both of us.

Pete was given a two-hour time slot every morning, sadly, this could be anytime between 6:30 am to 10 am, which meant I'd be getting up to let them in and keeping out of thier way, who needed a lie in any way.

We were given a bath chair to sit over the bath which would enable Pete to have a shower as and when he wanted.

I had sort of mastered an electric shaver, at least there would now be the chance of a proper shave, no more pointing out of all the bits I missed (which I did, often, who knew shaving someone else could be so difficult) and Pete would tell me the clothes he wanted to wear. I'd put them on the bed ready, at least one bit of control Pete still had.

I found it very hard, to give over Pete's morning routine to someone else. I hated it as much as he did. I felt I was failing him, but needs must and it was either this or staying in bed all day (not an option).

Thankfully, we are positive people and find humour where we probably shouldn’t, it is this that keeps us going and for the most part with a smile on our faces, to the outside world at least.

Two Weeks After Harvesting 16/04/2021

I thought I was just starting to get over my harvesting, not feeling quite as tired and starting to do a bit more pottering, then I went for my bone infusion, which on one hand was really good for the first time in all of my treatment, it actually took place in Basingstoke.

On the other, it made me even more tired than I was already and I am only now starting to get normal energy levels back (although I'm not sure what my normal energy levels are anymore).

I love having a clear head. I've just started driving again, only locally at the moment, but it's a start, I have lost a bit of weight and rarely have to wear my big girl pants as my normal ones now fit me.

My hair has finally stopped falling out and I've had my hair cut short (my hairdresser says, even though I felt I'd lost a lot of my hair because it was so thick in the first place, I've still got lots left, thanks Kirsty), this is in preparation for my transplant when I've been advised all of my hair will fall out, depending on when my date is, I may go even shorter on my hairstyle, but not totally sure about it yet.

I still can't remember things and forget things. Is that due to what's been going on with my body or an age-related thing, who knows? I'll blame the cancer anyway.

My left knee is still sore, I think I may need to get off my backside and walk more, it may help and at least, it isn't as painful as when I first started my treatment.

I couldn't even walk on it then and my stomach was all over the place, whatever I eat unsettles it, still not as bad as the constipation I had during my six months of treatment which is always a bonus.

I am feeling much better in myself, more like me, and I look normal (no puffer fish face), no one would think I was ill, which I think is great.

I know I still have a long way to go. I'm not out of the woods yet. I need to listen to my body and learn to live with the myeloma as best I can. Life is for living and I intend to enjoy every minute of it.

Pete is now the proud owner of a lovely purple electric wheelchair, it's second-hand, but who cares, it works (it would have been months to get a brand new one).

On our first outing, going out for a little amble around the local area, Pete managed to drop the chair off of the path so he was hanging half off the path into the road (he sat in the chair laughing), an elderly gentleman with a walking stick was the first to come to our rescue quickly followed by staff from the doctor's surgery (of which we were directly outside).

Much huffing and heaving and Pete was soon back on the path, none the worse for the incident. I couldn't stop laughing, once I knew he was okay, obviously.

At least, we knew Pete couldn't use that pathway again and we also found out some of the railings across the paths were very close, causing Pete to smash into them. This over time, resulted in calls to wheelchair services as the callipers on the chair would stop working properly (they enabled Pete to raise his legs to whatever level he wanted).

Pete did make contact with a local councillor and walked him around the area showing him the problems he had with accessibility, sadly, nothing was ever done.

Pete also took delivery of a raiser recliner chair, which made his life so much easier for getting in/out of a chair, it did mean our living room wasn't big enough to accommodate it. Thankfully, Pete's mum had room in her house to put our recliner chair, so one chair replaced the other.

On his regular respiratory appointments in Southampton, Pete was given a CPAP machine to help him breathe at night or during the day if he needed it. He didn't need it much at the moment but he would going forward (a mask sits over Pete's face which is then attached to the machine).

The therapy team were constantly monitoring Pete, checking his meds, he had physio and chair yoga and if I was worried or needed advice, there was a number I could call.

If that wasn't enough, the work on re-vamping the kitchen started, a makeshift kitchen was put in the living room and food deliveries were kept very busy. I tried my hand at a BBQ with a small disposable one used, food was not bad, sadly, the same couldn't be said about the small wooden table I'd used.

I'd inadvertently burnt a rather large hole in it. Oops, a new table is required and a lesson to probably not let me near another BBQ. Oh well. Thankfully, the kitchen was completed by the end of April (not without issues, but all sorted), and the boiler was condemned and replaced, life is certainly never dull.

Pete's running club (hatch Warren Runners, or Hatchies) decided to hold a charity event to raise money for MND in the form of a 24-hour relay running event, they called it Miles for Styles, it was supported by the local pub, running from one pub to another via our home (during the day).

Pete did the first and last laps on his mobility scooter, and Cheryl and Phil ran, it was well attended, raised a nice amount (I can't remember the exact amount) for MND and made it into the local paper. Again, so humbling to see the support and love Pete had from family and friends.

Oops
05/05/2021

I've been trying to write my blog for over a week with no way of seemingly starting a new post. I know I'm a real technophobe, so either my grandson has sorted it out for me or I just haven't been signing in properly (more than likely the latter).

I'm really pleased to say I'm feeling really good at the moment, yes my knee is sore, my eyebrows are sprouting all over the place, I get a little tired and my back gets very sore at times. My blood is still good with no infection showing at the moment.

I'm sleeping much better now, most of the meds are out of my system and I feel more like me. Sadly, I still forget most things and I can't remember much, is that due to the cancer treatment or my age, who knows?

I had my monthly bone-strengthening infusion yesterday, it's strange only going to the Rainbow unit once a month, after spending seemingly ages going every week and for the first time I felt able to drive myself to the treatment, that's only because it's in Basingstoke not Winchester, but still a step in the right direction.

I have my kidney, heart and lung tests next week in Southampton, assuming they're all fine, my transplant date shouldn't be far away. All seems a bit scary and real now.

It's a good job, I'm feeling pretty good as our house has been in chaos more or less since we moved in, thankfully, the end is in sight with most of the work and bits that needed doing almost done. It will be so nice to finally get the house to ourselves and to sort things at my pace, chaos a thing of the past.

Live life, love life and laugh. I am very good.

Pete's ability to do everyday tasks diminishes. It seems almost daily, he gets frustrated but never complains. I cannot attend hospital appointments with him, so Cheryl takes him, which is good as she asks questions I wouldn't even think or remember to ask (my woolly head frustrates me at times).

I can and do attend the clinics at the local hospice when Pete is invited, but we have to get dial a ride (local community bus that accommodates wheelchairs) or get one of the kids to drive us, using the small mobility scooter instead of the electric wheelchair.

Tests Done
15/05/2021

After saying I felt great and everything was going well, the same evening hubby dropped the remote and I couldn't get to it resulting in a meltdown from me, crying and sobbing, all over a TV remote. Just goes to show when you think everything is good it doesn't necessarily take much to flip things around. The remote was retrieved and I was fine.

I never realised how tired my infusion made me. I knew it made my bones ache, but the tiredness, sort of, got lost with the cocktail of other drugs I was on now, when I'm on minimum drugs I really feel it. As with everything I do, I am learning to listen and take it easy (most of the time).

On Monday and Tuesday, my tests were booked to make sure everything was in working order for my transplant. Monday was kidney and heart and Tuesday was blood and lung. Turning up at the Nuclear Medicine Department first thing Monday morning was a bit daunting, put at ease by a very nice man, a small dose of radiation was injected into my blood, and then I had to wait two hours before my first blood test.

The very nice man then showed us to the area where I would get my lung test and advised us to see if they could fit my test in today, he also said he would see what blood tests I needed and do them for me.

My name and phone number were left at the lung reception and we went off to grab a drink and have a little explore (what else do you do when there is the best part of two hours to fill).

As we arrived back in the waiting area of Nuclear Medicine for my first blood test, the mobile went off, it was the lung reception, they could squeeze me in for my tests, first blood was taken, and then we went straight to the lung waiting area where we were met by a man wearing what looked like a beekeepers suit (it was actually a protection suit with breathing apparatus).

Numerous breathing tests were then carried out, including one where I had to breathe in pure oxygen, which made me feel a little weird, but no time to spare as we were due back in Nuclear Medicine for my next blood test.

This time, the nice man took what he needed plus blood for my other tests, this meant I wouldn't need to return the next day. As we left Nuclear Medicine, we popped to the heart testing reception to see if I could bring my appointment forward.

Another nice man said all the appointment slots were full, if there was a cancellation I could go earlier but he wouldn't know until later, so it would be best to come back once all of my blood tests were finished.

Time for some lunch and a bit of fresh air before returning to Nuclear Medicine for my final blood test, all done and a quick return to heart testing reception, but no luck with moving my appointment forward, so time for a much-needed cuppa.

I wasn't feeling great at this point, so I reckon it's just what was needed (I could drink whilst having my kidney test but no caffeine, so no tea).

Sitting quietly whilst drinking my tea did help me to feel better, and then it was back to the heart testing area, the test didn't take as long as anticipated and we actually left the hospital by 4 pm. We'd been there for around seven hours, exhausting, but worth it as all my tests were done and dusted in one day.

A lovely day trip to Southampton, resulting in us managing to get all of the necessary tests done in one day instead of having to go back again, this meant Pete only had one day of someone from the care agency being with him when I was out as I didn't like him to be left on his own (Pete hated the thought of someone else having to be with him).

It was always a sweat when I went for my blood tests or infusions that Pete would be okay whilst I was out, usually, I wasn't long so it wasn't an issue, but I would get friends or family to pop in, just in case.

Still No Date 04/06/2021

After a phone catch-up with my consultant from Southampton, they are apparently still playing catch up from the pandemic and he doesn't anticipate me going in for my transplant until middle to end of June, even possibly early July.

The results of all the tests I had during my day out in Southampton Hospital were good, except my lung function is a little low, but it's nothing to worry about. To be fair, I'm quite happy with waiting as it means I can continue to enjoy my better health, as long as I listen to my body and take things easy.

In between, the lovely rain we're experiencing at the moment, I'm trying to get myself out and about, walking more to improve my fitness and lung capacity. Sadly, I don't fancy getting soaked, so I haven't been out as much as I'd hoped, fingers crossed, that we finally get some much-needed sunshine and I'll be happy to walk more.

As is quite normal with me, I get distracted very easily and here we are, well over a week later, and I've just realised I never finished my blog, which is quite handy as I've also had my monthly catch-up with Dr Noel.

He still continues to make me chuckle as he'll call me as soon as he sees my blood results, so I got a call late on Wednesday afternoon instead of Friday morning, results are still very positive, and levels are all low, just where they need to be.

Dr Noel was surprised, I'd still not got a hospital date, but there wasn't anything anyone could do except wait, he did say I'd come out of the hospital with a big bag of meds (thought I'd left those days behind when I finished my six months of chemo) including an inhaler, that doesn't sound good, but I guess I'll be enlightened when I get the transplant done.

Apparently, once I go into hospital, I'm under the care of the Southampton consultant and Dr Noel picks up my care again six weeks after coming out of hospital. I actually had a little flutter of anxiety at the thought of Dr Noel not looking after me, but it's only for a short time, I'm sure everything will be fine.

In the space of starting writing and actually finishing it, I've even had another infusion of my bone-strengthening stuff (I may have also gotten distracted by the few days of lovely sunshine) and I feel shattered today.

So, I'll be mostly resting and chilling, sadly indoors as it's peeing with rain at the moment and even our newly installed awning will not entice me outside (I don't mind being shaded from the sun as I can still feel the warmth, I'm not sure how shower proof the awning is. I don't fancy testing it out and it's too cold).

Both of my knees are quite sore at the moment, and the pain interrupts my sleep along with achy legs. I do manage to get back to sleep and I'm sure it'll all sort itself out. My back aches a lot and the things I do as part of my daily life that involve too much exertion on my arms actually cause pain across my back/shoulders.

I may not feel the pain initially, but it hits later, which is where I cause myself problems as I've not realised my body hasn't coped with what I've been doing. We now have a cleaner, which I'm not happy about but I do realise I need the help.

I have to look after myself and my body. I have to choose my battles to help me and make my life easier. It has taken a while for me to get to this point and it isn't easy. I'm still learning and I guess, I will always be.

I am good, I am happy, be safe and enjoy life.

Pete was still moving around with the aid of the Zimmer but his legs were getting increasingly wobbly, he went into our bathroom one morning, wobbled and then slid down the bathroom door, he wasn't hurt but I couldn't move him and he was incapable of moving himself, scared the life out of both of us and brought home how vulnerable he was.

Thankfully, his carer was due anytime to get him washed and dressed, even though he wasn't supposed to (manual handling rules) he arrived and got Pete up with no problem, there is no answer or solution to this Pete just needs to be more careful.

Pete was also struggling to get himself up off of the stairlift, downstairs wasn't an issue, it was at night when going to bed, if Liv was around it was easier as she had the strength to steady the Zimmer frame to enable Pete to pull himself up. I, sadly did not, but would do whatever I needed to get him up.

I tried a handling belt, which worked for a while. I was always petrified of him tumbling down the stairs, thankfully, he never did, whatever or, however, we did, we always managed to get him up.

I also struggled to lift his legs into bed at night (they seemed literally like dead weights), a conversation with one of the therapy team resulted in some sort of leg lift being fitted to his bed. For whatever reason, Pete was extra wobbly when going to bed on this particular evening and panicked when he got off the stair lift.

Thankfully, my friend Donna was still here (they had watched an Arsenal match together), she came up to help calm Pete whilst I ran downstairs, brought up the perch stool, and shoved it under Pete which allowed him to rest in between taking a few steps with the Zimmer frame.

We finally managed to get him into the bedroom, then tried using the leg lift, oh my goodness, there wasn't enough clearance between the bed rail and bed to get his legs on, much huffing and puffing and much laughter, we decided the leg lift needed to come off.

Pete was safely perched on the bed, so Donna and I worked around him, no easy feat but we managed to remove it and I got Pete comfortable in bed. Thankful for Donna's help and input, needless to say, the leg lift was returned as soon as possible.

Pete also took the decision to stop driving, he was struggling and was even possibly becoming unsafe. We tried very hard to get him into one of the passenger seats in the Mercedes due to his right side being almost non-cooperative to any form of movement and not being able to get his legs into the car.

We were left with no form of transport, except for dial a ride, community transport, good old-fashioned buses or Pete taking himself off in his electric wheelchair.

The joys of public transport or buses was very short-lived, if you've ever seen 'The Inbetweeners', you'll know the reference I'm about to mention.

Pete referred to us (laughingly) as 'bus W****ks', why was it short-lived, we discovered that if there were no baby buggies onboard, Pete could comfortably manoeuvre himself into the required space and out again; when a buggy was occupying the space next to him, he couldn't get himself out, especially when the said buggy owner wouldn't move out of the way for him.

I actually got off the bus and the driver unknowingly almost drove off with Pete still onboard, struggling to get off; needless to say, it freaked Pete out and he refused to get on another bus.

It meant I had to take over, the running around of Liv; thankfully, her driving test was due very soon, fingers crossed she'd pass and at least, that would be one less thing to worry about.

As I was no longer having chemo, only regular bone-strengthening infusions, the medication I needed to take was now reduced, my head was no longer woolly (my memory was pants, chemo brain or age) and my body was returning to nearer its normal size.

I felt confident to drive again, at least locally. Our local pub was close by, easy enough in both distance and safe for Pete to use his wheelchair, we had many a chilled stroll through the park (still having frequent run-ins with the barriers across many of the paths, resulting in calls to wheelchair services to get the wheelchair sorted) and of course, ending up in the pub for a cheeky beverage or two.

This helped Pete keep his independence as he was also able to take himself to meet friends in the pub. It also meant, on more than one occasion, Pete would arrive home a little merry (someone always walked home with him) and the joys of getting his wheelchair through our narrow hall was a sight to watch, resulting in much laughter and one or two scrapes along the wall.

Now, the search was on to find a mode of transport suitable for Pete and his wheelchair and that I was comfortable driving, or could drive. Where on Earth do I start? No one seems to be able to give me any information or guidance, so it's down to me and the good old internet.

I googled wheelchair-accessible vehicle dealerships (WAVs for short), thankfully, my second call resulted in a very helpful dealership and man in the Midlands, he asked lots of questions and needed some measurements, including the size of the wheelchair and how high Pete's head was above the wheelchair headrest.

Due to the size of the wheelchair and Pete's height the only vehicle suitable was a converted VW Caravelle, flipping heck. Was it something I was even going to be comfortable driving?

It was arranged for the van to be driven, down from the Midlands (there were still lots of restrictions due to COVID), if Pete's chair didn't fit or I wasn't able to drive it, then it would be taken back, a win-win situation for us. The van and man arrived, and he set up the securing front straps for the wheelchair so we wouldn't need to alter them.

I was shown how to secure Pete in the back, he climbed in the front passenger seat and I very apprehensively climbed up into the driver's seat. Wow, it was a lot easier to drive than I imagined.

I was higher up (great for a vertically challenged person like me) and had a much better view of everything and it was surprisingly light to steer. Reversing, and height restrictions all checked out. Pete was happy (I'll have to remember to take it slower around comers as Pete gets flung around quite easily).

I was happy, and the van was sold (phew). All paperwork completed. I dropped the man at the train station, all that was left was to sell the Mercedes. That would be Pete's job over the next few days. Pete is mobile again, happy us.

Liv passed her test and put the flags out, yeah, we need to get her car as soon as possible, no mean feat during lockdown and the fact she could only drive an automatic.

Auto trader gave us a car trader not too far away who would deliver a car for us to check over, a little Toyota Aygo was quickly purchased and Liv was independent, no more running her around (in fact, her first trip out was driving a flatmate to Luton airport, fair play to her).

We had a visit from the peg nurse to discuss Pete having a peg (feeding tube) fitted, he didn't need it at the moment but whilst he was relatively fit and well, it was often advised to have it done. Pete had initially been against having one fitted, so this was a really positive step that he was even willing to have a conversation about it and a big relief to me.

Going forward when he would struggle to swallow, which would affect his ability to eat, drink or take medication, he would be able to have it all via the peg.

Another discussion with the therapy team about Pete's mobility, the difficulty of getting off of the stairlift and his fear of falling when moving upstairs resulted in the decision to move Pete's bed downstairs.

It literally happened in less than 24 hours. We had to give the fish tank away that night, have the comer piece of our sofa removed to Pete's mum's for storage and consider how Pete was going to get my attention at night as he couldn't call out whilst wearing the CPAP machine.

The bed was set up downstairs and I spent the first week sleeping on the sofa, in case, Pete needed me and I didn't want to sleep upstairs on my own. This was not good for me or my body, I didn't sleep well and my back was so sore, we did buy a bell and a mobile holder that enabled Pete to call me in the night (he still had mobility in his left hand).

I plugged the bell receiver upstairs in the bedroom, turned the sound down so it wouldn't scare the life out of me and with the help of my sister, we moved the bedroom around to make it a bit easier to actually sleep upstairs.

I wasn't ready to get the double bed back yet, although my bed was small (especially as the cat decided to share it with me) it was easier than contemplating sleeping in our double bed on my own.

Needless to say, many tears were shed those first few nights, in between running up and down stairs if the CPAP machine alarmed (which it often did at night) or Pete rang the bell because he needed a wee or something else. Another milestone, I'd rather not have reached as MND was not even very slowly taking my husband away from me.

Pete's morning care routine, now increased to two carers to wash and get him up (sadly, there was no shower downstairs) in the morning and two in the evening to put him to bed, again timings were rubbish, and he could still have an early morning call and could be put to bed anytime from 7:30–9:30 pm no time at all for someone in their early 50s. This caused many tears and much frustration for Pete.

The first morning Pete was downstairs, and I was upstairs, I heard him say, "Don't leave me as I can't stand for long."

The next moment, there was a crash. I ran down the stairs and Pete was on the floor, thankfully not hurt but extremely cross and frustrated, he was still very vocal at this moment in time.

So, how do we get him up off of the floor, the male carer was useless and just stood there. I looked around the room, if we could get Pete onto the poofy, we then might be able to get him to use his Zimmer to stand up with our help, the carers moved the poofy near to Pete, he had very little upper body strength so would be reliant on us gently helping him.

Between the three of us, Pete doing what he could, we managed to get him onto the poofy, a little rest, then with a lot of help from us, Pete was standing, a little shuffle to his chair, he was shaken up but okay, feet up and chill for Pete.

The carers were late leaving. I don't care, he should've listened to Pete. I'm so mad at them. Pete could've been hurt, and my body was now hurting and it all could've been avoided. Not exactly installing confidence in Pete for future care. I did call the care agencies and tell them, I'm not sure he (the carer) would report it (apparently, he did a few days later).

I brought Pete a cover for him and his wheelchair, after all our good old British weather is so unpredictable. I wanted him to stay dry and the electrics on the wheelchair to be protected.

Pete used it only once, he said he looked like a condom and felt like a right prat (to be fair he did look like a condom) and I couldn't help laughing at him.

St Michael's Hospice offered reflexology or massage to Pete and as his wife, I was also allowed to have these lovely sessions. Pete usually had reflexology, I had a neck and back massage. I drove us to the sessions, it was a nice chance for both of us to have a little bit of *me* time, very relaxing, enjoyable and much needed.

After Pete's visit from the peg nurse (which seemed like weeks ago), he had come to the decision he would go ahead and have a peg fitted. A date was arranged towards the end of July, he was assured he would be looked after and all his needs met during his hospital stay of hopefully two nights.

I couldn't go with him to the hospital or visit due to my vulnerability and low immunity. Cheryl took him in, Liv dropped some stuff off for him, needless to say when he was picked up after having the peg put in he wasn't a happy bunny.

He had spent a lot of time on his own, and no one came to help him eat, so he hadn't eaten much and he vowed never to go near a hospital again. It turns out, someone could have been with him, but we were never told!

With everything else going on in our lives, we decided to add even more to it and have the downstairs, stairs and landing decorated, glutens for punishment or what. Thankfully, Pete's electric wheelchair can elevate his legs and tilt back, so he was quite comfortable outside in that.

We did have to use the *condom* cover a few times for him due to the weather conditions and much to his annoyance. The iPad, his side table and all sorts of bits and pieces were taken outside to aid with our comfort, almost like our camping trips, but I think more like glamping as we had everything within reach.

We had an awning installed when the garden was revamped, so that I could sit outside in the shade during the summer months, this was more a blessing from the rain sadly rather than the sun.

Pete was still able to speak relatively clearly but his voice was getting quieter, he was advised to *bank* his voice for future use, as can be imagined Pete initially refused point-blank to even contemplate it.

Going forward Pete would have access to a computer that he would be able to work with his eyes if his voice was banked we'd be able to hear his voice rather than the computers, after much persuasion and bribing Pete finally agreed to bank his voice.

Turns out it was really easy, he had to read some lines from a chosen story on a special site we were given and that was it. Amazing what technology can do, when we heard the results it had corrected some of the speech Pete had already lost, if he hadn't been so stubborn and waited his voice recording would have been a perfect copy.

I had a big birthday coming up, and with everything going on in our lives, it wasn't even on my radar. Pete happened to ask what I might like.

To be honest, I had no idea, but out of my mouth came, "Maybe, a tandem parachute jump."

I hadn't really enjoyed the indoor skydiving session I'd done, never mind doing it for real, whatever was I thinking. I didn't really think much about it then, a few days later, Pete asked if I wanted photos as well.

"May as well as I'll not do it again," was my reply.

Still, not thinking too much about it, then *all booked* and there it was. I was doing a skydive in a few weeks' time!

Pete decided he wanted to buy those close to him something to remember him by, so a family trip to the jewellers was arranged. I felt a bit overwhelmed and must admit to shedding a few tears.

Pete, on the other hand, was in his element, maybe fuelled by the free glass (or two) of bubbly, he knew what he wanted, and with a little guidance and input from all of us, purchases were made and everything ordered.

All in all, a successful shopping trip, be it a bit emotional (for me anyway).

(Pete had a couple of life insurance policies, one of which included a critical illness policy. The life insurance/critical illness policy paid out, but the other one would only pay out if Pete had less than a year to live! This payout enabled us to pay off what was left of our mortgage, definitely giving us peace of mind and with some leftover to make our lives a little easier).

Keeping Pete out and about was certainly easier with the van, his mate Steve was happy to drive him places as were Cheryl, Phil and myself, this enabled Pete to keep an active social life and go out and about.

It was dependent on who was driving as to how much Pete was flung around in the back, much to his amusement! He decided a trip down to the sea and the designer outlet at Gunwharf Keys was in order. Steve drove, a few purchases were made but more importantly, a few cocktails on the seafront, were very much enjoyed by Pete and the sun actually came out.

One Year Ago 24/08/2021

One year ago today, I was given my diagnosis of multiple myeloma, doesn't seem possible and doesn't time fly when you're having fun! I can't believe, it's been so long since my last post either, so let's see what's been going on.

I still have no date for my transplant even though there was a bit of excitement generated from my Southampton consultation in July where he thought I might be having it at the end of August and was going to go through my consent form when he spoke to me mid-way through the month.

Sadly, it wasn't to be and I'm no nearer to getting a date, possibly end of September, who knows, they're still apparently playing catch-up. I may be lucky with a date at my next consultation on 21 September. I'll just have to wait and see. To me, it means, I'm still able to get out and about and enjoy the summer (even if there isn't much sun).

I am still in good health and my blood results are still amazing. Yes, my knees still play me up, my back still gives me pain, some days more than others and my limbs are more achy, especially at night (a couple of paracetamol before bed helps).

I'm still having my monthly infusion which seems to knock me out for a few days and makes me very emotional and I'm still on my holding meds, considering everything I'm doing pretty well.

The upheaval of sorting a new house into a home is finally over, apart from needing to bring some unopened boxes down from the loft to sort. I think we're finally there. From re-vamping the garden, a small kitchen makeover that turned into a nightmare and ended up into more of a major overhaul, furniture constantly being moved around and finally decorating. I can happily say, we now have a lovely new home.

Constant medical appointments, blood tests and consultations for me and hubby are a constant juggling act and certainly keep me on my toes. The added bonus of a neck/shoulder/back massage, every now and then, is sheer bliss and much needed (thank you to the team at St Micheal's Hospice).

As ever the constant support, love and help from family and friends is very much needed, appreciated and helps keep me going forward. I have lots to do, places to go, people to see and a skydive to do next month (thanks hubby) fingers crossed, my medical team agree I'm okay to do it. Life is tough at times but it is also good. I'm happy and well. Be safe, be happy, be kind to each other.

A very misty day and I was off to Salisbury to do my skydive. Was I nervous? Surprisingly enough, I wasn't (not at this point anyway). Steve drove as I wasn't comfortable driving the van any distance.

Pete's mum joined us and we set off for the airfield. Thankfully by the time we set off, the mist had lifted leaving a beautiful (very hot) sunny day. Due to the weather, the jumps were running well behind time, why they didn't phone and delay our start time is beyond me as we waited and waited and waited.

Poor Pete was getting uncomfortable in his chair, he wanted to stand up, but due to the lack of facilities I dared not let him, at least, they had a disabled toilet he could use. He was in the sun, then inside out of the sun, then back out, bored, frustrated (that was just me) and finally, after five hours of waiting I was called for my training.

Finally, it was going to happen, it suddenly became very real. I was still quite calm as I went through my training. I was put into my parachute and then introduced to a nice young man who I was going to be attached to for the jump. Still, feeling very calm.

I wandered back to Pete to wait for my flight to be called. We were given the go-ahead, and I gave Pete a big hug. I was feeling quite excited, and the group going in my jump gathered together and we headed to the small plane, still feeling very calm. We all shuffled to our places, quite hard to do when you're attached to another human being.

Then, we were bumping along the grass (runway), and were airborne, as we climbed higher. I sat listening to the others expressing their fear and watching the look on their faces, still unbelievably calm. Then, it was my turn, and only as I sat with my feet hanging out of the plane did I think, *Oh shite*.

Then, we were falling, wow what an amazing experience, the world stretched out before us (not really, but I could see for miles), the peace, except for my cheeks wobbling like I don't know what and not being able to catch my breath for the briefest of time, then the parachute was opened.

It was the very best of feelings, floating gently down to earth, I was asked if I'd like to be twisted around to see all around us, of course, I did. After all, I had to make the most of my time in the sky. What I didn't realise was how painful all the twisting around was.

I had bruises on my chest and the tops of my legs where the straps had been, for days after, but it was so worth it. All too quickly, we were down and landing with a gentle bump. It had taken six and a half hours (five hours of waiting) to get back on the ground and finally, head home, but WOW, I had a smile on my face for days and the memory forever.

Pete's mobility had again taken a bit of a nosedive, he struggled to bear weight, and he could no longer get into the toilet (even though we'd had a posh loo fitted not that long ago that self-flushed and gave a wash and dry to help going to the loo easier) and much to his frustration had to use a commode.

I did try dragging him to the toilet whilst sitting on the commode as it did fit over the toilet, but with so much huffing, puffing and struggling, I sadly just couldn't do it. Often resulting in tears on my part as I felt I was letting Pete down and tears on Pete's part as he felt guilty for putting me through this, it was just shite.

There was also the fact if he needed to go, my trying to drag him to the toilet took too long and the decision was made to just use the commode, another erosion of Pete's independence and dignity.

With the help of his riser, recliner chair, we could get Pete to a standing position, if the commode was positioned next to the chair, with the aid of his walking frame he was just about able to shuffle onto the commode, that was the easy part, getting him off again was a feat in itself and I struggled big time.

Even though I was in relatively good health, waiting for my transplant, my bones still hurt, my back in particular if I did too much, helping. Pete wasn't helping me at all but I wouldn't change it for the world, in my eyes Pete had it a lot worse than me.

I'll do anything and everything to make things easier for him, no matter the price I pay in pain. After another conversation with the therapy team, it was decided that Pete now needed a hoist to help get in/out of bed, to put him onto the commode and into the wheelchair.

It was agreed to have a H-hoist fitted (looks a bit like a rugby goalpost), it was to go between the bed and his riser/recliner chair. Thankfully, due to my job, I had training on hoisting people and knew what to do. Once I'd been shown which straps to use on his sling, I knew that I was good to go (and often showed the carers what to do).

If I was on my own and using the hoist, I'd pull the chair over to the hoist so that it was easier to manoeuvre Pete into it, although the hoist certainly made life easier, it wasn't versatile enough for all of Pete's needs. One time, I hoisted Pete out of the chair, it was fully reclined, I pressed the remote to sit it back up and it didn't move, panic set in.

What am I going to do if the chair won't work, it's Pete's lifeline, once Pete was safely on his bed, I then got on the floor and started feeling around it turns out the power cable had come adrift, thank goodness, something I could fix myself, panic over.

The call came from the jewellers that everything was all gifted wrapped and ready for collection, off we trotted, another excursion into town, another complimentary glass of bubbly and, of course, another visit to a pub for a pint or two.

I was given the task of writing cards to go with the said gifts, dictated by Pete, very emotional for both of us. I tried very hard not to let tears fall onto the cards and smudge my writing and I think I spent more time mopping both our tears over the next few hours than actually writing.

Phew job done, all cards were written and placed with appropriate gifts. Pete's mates were due round, a very emotional evening, lots of tears, lots of hugs, lots of laughter, lots of love and, of course, lots of alcohol.

I put Pete to bed myself that night, just so he could be normal and go to bed late, he was more than a little hungover the next morning, but what a night and, of course, beautiful memories made.

Pete needed to get himself together as his family were due over that afternoon, more a tea and cake thing, but still with the availability of alcohol if wanted. Again, a very emotional time, with more tears, laughter, hugs and love, job done.

I was emotionally exhausted, and I guess Pete was too, he never said. In fact, he rarely showed his true emotions, but I could see so much in his eyes and body language, that broke my heart that I couldn't do anything to make it better, except follow his wishes.

Thank goodness for modem technology, environmental services came out and did goodness knows what to link up Pete's iPad to enable him to control the TV, music, lights and a few other things. He was still just about able to use his left hand and could touch the screen to make it work if we put it in a holder near him, another plus for continued independence.

An eye gaze computer was also given to Pete, it had his voice already installed from when he'd banked it a few months earlier. Pete wasn't happy and refused point-blank to use it, he was still able to use his voice (just about) so I guess thought he didn't need it.

There really was no point trying to force Pete to do something he didn't want to, it was going to have to be an ongoing, gentle persuasive battle with him.

With my stem cell transplant now being imminent, we had to think about Pete's care whilst I was in hospital and the fact I'd not be able to do very much once I was home, as well as the possibility, that I may initially need some help.

Again, the therapy team were invaluable in their support and a live-in carer was arranged. Liv was now at uni in London (bless her she had to drive herself to London and move herself into her uni flat, a braver person than me to drive in London) so wasn't home much and we had a spare room.

I must admit to being a little unsure of the idea, of a total stranger sharing our home and also handing Pete's full care over to someone else, sadly there was no alternative.

The carer was due to arrive the day before my hospital admission so that he could familiarise himself with Pete's routine and all the medication he required, best-laid plans and all, my hospital admission was brought forward by 24 hours.

I hadn't even packed my bag, never mind shaving my hair (going through all of the cancer treatment didn't bother me, losing my hair did), I'd rather have my hair shaved off than wake up to clumps of it on my pillow.

I also had to spend some time at Basingstoke Hospital having a PICC line inserted before I could be admitted to Southampton, a very manic few hours and frantic phone calls to the care agency to get the carer here earlier if possible.

Sadly, they didn't arrive before I had to leave, so I left the familiarisation stuff to Phil and Cheryl (once she'd deposited me at Southampton), there are no words to express how I felt about leaving Pete, how he'd get on with a stranger looking after him (thankful his speech could just about be understood) or if he would have deteriorated even more during my absence, never mind even thinking about what lay ahead of me! Great distraction, I guess.

The first couple of days during my hospital stay were, to say the least, very intense and unbeknown to me there were issues with the live-in carer, who couldn't seem to grasp Pete's medication, thankfully, the kids were keeping a very watchful eye on the situation and the carer was very quickly replaced.

He seemed much more capable and every time Pete and I Facetimed during my hospitalisation, I was pleased to see Pete well cared for, happy and relaxed. Pete had a respiratory clinic appointment at Southampton Hospital whilst I was there and I'd asked if Pete could come visit me.

Due to the COVID restrictions and the fact I was now extremely vulnerable to any germs as my immunity had been wiped out by the high dose of chemo, I was told no.

Happily, Cheryl ignored that and bought Pete to see me, they weren't allowed in the room but could stand in the doorway, tears were shed by both myself and Pete, it was so lovely to see him (and Cheryl of course), made me realise how much I was missing home.

Pete was still employed and a meeting was arranged for his boss and personnel to visit him whilst I was in hospital, thankfully Cheryl and Phil were around, they had not realised how much Pete's mobility had deteriorated (I think they were quite shocked) they gave him an area to work that was a few hours' drive away, which Pete was clearly incapable of doing.

(Cheryl and Phil think they were trying to oust him from his job). After that, Pete was put on permanent sick leave and well looked after by his company (we'll never know what the true intentions of that visit were), a big relief for both of us.

Whilst I was hospitalised, Cheryl took Pete up to London for a visit to the Shard (life carries on as normal). Liv joined them and I must admit to being more than a little jealous when I saw the photos, but also glad that Pete was still getting out and about and more importantly, enjoying himself.

It's Finally Happened 22/10/2021

A little over three weeks ago, I arrived at Southampton Hospital. I was initially given a date, which was almost immediately changed, so I thought, I wouldn't jinx anything and kept quiet. I had my COVID test and was then asked to go to the Rainbow Unit in Basingstoke, where I received my treatment to get a PICC line fitted and to call Southampton once it was in.

I thought it would be a quick in and out of the unit, hour and a half later, feeling a little groggy I emerged thankfully eldest daughter had the foresight to realise I'd probably not feel like driving myself and even managed to get some fuel for the van whilst she waited.

I never realised (obviously) how invasive a PICC line was and what it entailed to fit it (I wonder how easy it is to take it out). By the time we got home, it was almost lunchtime. I made the call to Southampton only to be told my bed's ready now, talk about panic-stricken, my date was for 1 October.

I hadn't even packed, hadn't shaved my hair, didn't know when hubby's carer was arriving and…breathe. Call to care agency, carer was on his way, call to hospital to say I'd be there around 4 pm, sit and have my hair shaved.

Carer arrives, a quick tour and what's what for him to do whilst the kids pack my case and then it's time to go. Never have I felt such a mixed bag of emotions, fear, worry, sadness, loneliness and helplessness as I left home, no idea of how long I'd be gone and what was ahead.

Since my diagnosis, I am really on my own, this is about me and finally facing up to my cancer, no more hiding it wasn't a nice feeling, as I couldn't do anything about it, just faced it and got on with it.

On 30 September, I arrived for my next round of treatment, case unpacked, eldest leaves and probably, for the first time, it's just me in my room, on my own, but with the knowledge of so much love and support from my beloved family and friends to see me through.

No visitors were initially allowed due to my vulnerability as I started my treatment. The next day, I have a high dose of chemo, lots of ice pops to try to reduce the mouth ulcers and soreness associated with it and lots of mouthwashes.

Saturday, 2 October is the return of my bone marrow, I watch as my bone marrow is warmed in a small bath of water to defrost it and is then returned to me via an IV line. I feel no pain, no discomfort and am frequently checked to make sure everything is okay. Apparently, the room smelt like sweet corn and did for days after, but I never did smell it.

The next few weeks are a blur of sleeping, sleeping and more sleeping. In between, was a very dry mouth but thankfully no ulcers, diarrhoea, a constant retching and feeling sick and then my hair started falling out, that did bring a few tears and a kind nurse shaved more of my hair off.

My temperature also decided to yo-yo, weirdly most nights, which resulted in strong antibiotics, it has only just started to behave and no real cause for it was ever found.

Three weeks into my stay and I can feel myself slowly getting stronger. I'm sleeping less and I'm trying to take an interest in my food, which isn't easy when it's hospital food (yuk). I'm on a specialist diet and I've also got my silly eating issues, breakfast is rice crispies followed by a slice of jam on toast (toast is always cold), and lunch is usually a ham sandwich.

I've tried adding a plate of chips, which I couldn't chew, so, I'm trying some rice instead. Tea is a plain jacket potato, I've tried adding beans (they were so dried up they stuck to the plate) and tuna mayonnaise (made me ill). I have a real want for cauliflower, I can have cauliflower cheese, but not just cauliflower as it's not on the menu.

Funny, the things you crave when you can't have them. My appetite isn't great and I rarely eat all I'm given, at least, I'm managing to eat some of it. Being in your own room with en suite is a big advantage.

I'm down the end of a corridor, so it's really quiet, sadly it also means I feel really isolated and lonely. More so this week, as I've started to feel better and I'm awake more. The staff are fantastic but also very busy, so don't really have time to chat.

Am I ready to go home? You bet. Do I know when I going home? Not yet. Hopefully, it shouldn't be too long as my temperature is now under control and so is the sickness.

What will it mean when I do go home? I'll be extremely tired and extremely vulnerable, even a cold could put me in the hospital, never mind any other germs or bugs.

In preparation for my hospitalisation, the continual decline in Pete's health and the fact he was waking a lot during the night for various reasons (needing a wee, needing turning, CPAP machine alarming).

I was struggling big time to cope, lack of sleep at night and constantly worrying the lovely therapy team again stepped in and with the help of the care agency night carers were arranged, most of the nights were okay, but on occasion the night carer would fall asleep!

I could still hear Pete and the CPAP machine when it alarmed, if there didn't seem to be a response I'd come downstairs. I've had carers asleep stretched across the living room floor, sat on the sofa and on the kitchen chair, not great for Pete who hadn't wanted them in the first place but needs must (we also knew it wasn't uncommon for the night carers to have worked during the day!).

I would also come down if Pete was agitated and seemingly not settling, wearing the mask on his face meant he struggled even more to communicate his needs. I could usually understand him or reset the mask to stop it leaking (one of the reasons for the CPAP machine to alarm).

It was lovely to be home from hospital, and so great to have Pete come meet me with Cheryl, meant I was able to sit and hold his hand in the van on the way home, his speech had deteriorated even more, but then, I had noticed that during our calls, I hadn't asked how he was getting on with the eye gaze during our calls whilst I was away as he wasn't able to chat for long. so time was precious.

Walking into our home and meeting a person who to me was a stranger but to Pete was the person who had got to know him, his routine, taken care of him and got to know our family,

I almost felt like an outsider. To be fair even the journey home exhausted me.

I so wanted to go to bed, understandably Pete wanted me to spend some time downstairs with him. Pete had also given the carer some money to look after me for the first week, having a shower exhausted me, and I had to lay on the bed to recover (I was able to thankfully do it myself, I was very lucky to have an en suite in my bedroom so didn't have to share a bathroom) and my appetite was non-existent which meant I had no interest in food or cooking.

It was certainly going to take a bit of getting used to, but a must for a live-in carer, at this moment in time, I could hardly take care of myself, never mind looking after Pete.

My birthday (60th) was a few weeks after getting out of the hospital, my vulnerability and my get-up-and-go having gone, meant there were no big celebrations; to be honest, I was just glad to be home. I woke to someone having decorated the living room with banners and balloons and shared the day quietly with family.

I was nevertheless spoilt rotten with gifts, cards and messages from family and friends. We could celebrate properly at a later date.

Home Sweet Home
6/11/2021

Two weeks ago, on 23/10/21, after just under three and a half weeks in hospital, I was finally allowed home. Initially, due to my sickness and temperature yo-yoing, I'd been told I'd not be going home until early the following week, starting to feel better and not being able to have visitors I wasn't a happy bunny, but obviously there was no point coming home if my body wasn't ready.

My temperature suddenly seemed to sort itself out, so the doctors decided I could come home. I certainly wasn't going to argue with them. It's very surreal leaving the hospital after what seemed like an eternity, feeling fresh air on my face, a definite drop in temperature but an overall sense of freedom.

Arriving home and tackling stairs for the first time in a while was interesting, wobbly legs, huffing and puffing and that's just going up, never mind coming back down. It was just so nice to be home and sleeping in my own bed. Sadly, the nausea stayed with me and the anti-sickness meds didn't seem to do very much.

I still had very little appetite and then, I started being sick, resulting in a call to Southampton for some help. They changed my anti-sickness medication to the one I had during my initial treatment, but I didn't have much of it left and I was wondering how I was going to get some more.

Out of the blue, I got a call from Dr Noel checking in on me. Result? He prescribed some more medicine which I picked up when I went for my blood tests at the end of the week.

I am still feeling nauseous, but finally, it is starting to subside and I'm starting to reduce my anti-sickness meds. My appetite is still rubbish, my go-to meal is two fish fingers and I can now manage eight chips (as long as they're not too big), lunch is usually a ham sandwich and breakfast two slices of toast, sometimes, I can eat it all sometimes not.

I am finally managing to drink most of a small cup of tea, so long as it's weak. I'm drinking lemon squash, which I wouldn't usually touch (it masks the taste of cooled boiled water) and I'm back to drinking Pepsi Max but can't stomach other fizzy drinks.

My taste buds are definitely savoury-based at the moment and weird, my go-to snacks are plain crisps but they have to be walkers and I've definitely lost my sweet tooth (I'm sure it will return).

I can't bear the thought of roast chicken dinner at the moment due to trying one in the hospital and my cotton mouth made everything seem really dry and tasteless, needless to say after a mouthful I gave up.

My head is quite sensitive and I have to sleep wearing a chemo cap. I was thinking about re-shaving it to see if that would help but in the last few days, I have felt a fine covering of hair on my bald areas so I'm leaving well alone.

I still get worn out when I shower and find it strange having no hair to worry about. My skin is very crepey and dry, so I'm putting lots of moisturiser on it. I try to go out for a walk most days, going a little bit further each day and upstairs to the toilet rather than using the downstairs loo. I know it'll take a while, but everything will get easier, it'll just take time.

As I continued to get stronger, Pete sadly was not, the only mobility he had was in his left hand and his head, and his hand was slowly deteriorating, on the positive, he had mastered the eye gaze (after lots and lots of swearing and much frustration), such an amazing piece of kit.

Not only does it allow Pete to talk to us (yes, it was slow, which is only to be expected when you're using your eyes to write words and if you look at the screen whilst Pete is typing it messes with the words, which understandably frustrates him).

He is able to communicate on Facebook, WhatsApp, text messages and emails, he can do his own banking, plus a host of other things giving him so much independence and control which is just as well as I'm useless with technology which frustrated Pete to no end, especially when he wanted me to send messages for him.

Pete even has a detachable frame fitted to the wheelchair on which the eye gaze sits which means it can go everywhere with him and be able to communicate with everyone. On one of our many walks around the park, Pete suddenly stopped his wheelchair. I looked at him, he had tears streaming down his face and had started sobbing.

This wasn't good as it meant he struggled to catch his breath, which can be very scary for both of us. I needed to calm him down before I could find out was what wrong, looking into his eyes I got him to take deep breaths (as much as he could) and count with him, thankfully slowing his breathing and calming him.

Now, to find out what's wrong, "I don't want to be here anymore," were his words.

Now, I was crying (thankfully the park was empty), how on earth do I answer that? He was struggling to cope with what was happening to him, felt bad for what I did for him and that he could do nothing to help me.

I just stood hugging him, neither of us had chosen our illnesses and neither of us could change them, we needed to deal with it and get on with it the best way we could, some days, being so much harder than others.

I needed help to sort Pete's mindset out, with his permission I called the therapy team, and it was decided, the doctor would come out that day. When they arrived, I explained what had happened, and what Pete had said, then sat back and let the doctor talk to Pete.

He cried, so I cried (I hated it when he was upset), thankfully, he hadn't had enough, and was just struggling to cope. He was already on a very low dose of antidepressants, it was agreed the dose would be upped and monitored until he was in a better frame of mind (sigh of relief).

Pete has a constant round of people coming to the house, balloon changes for his rig, a chiropodist to keep his feet healthy (I'll happily keep his fingernails trimmed but not his feet), a therapy team, a doctor, wheelchair services, environmental services, speech and language, meds constantly being monitored and changed, all these people helping to keep Pete leading what is for him as normal a life as possible.

I can't even begin to imagine how it must feel for Pete, not so long ago, he was an active independent person, now, he is totally dependent on someone for everything, thank goodness for humour!

Friends and family often came to visit, sometimes staying for lunch, sometimes just for a cuppa and Pete still went out to the pub, sometimes Macca (Steve) drove him (and the carer) to town for a change of scenery.

Pete was also invited to a party with his running club (I was not) I didn't feel like driving, so Phil drove him (and his carer) we'd arranged for the night carer to come later, so Pete could have a very rare proper night out.

A rather merry but very happy Pete arrived home, looked after and supplied with alcohol by his lovely running harem no doubt, a hilarious 10 minutes or so of trying to get Pete through the front door without wrecking either the house or his chair, then the realisation of no night carer had turned up.

I helped get Pete out of the chair and hoisted onto his bed before calling the care agency, they said they'd call me back as soon as they'd found out what had happened. I returned to Pete and finished helping get him settled in bed.

I let the carer go to bed as there was no point in both of us being up, he said to call him if I needed anything, then a phone call to say our night carer had taken the night off but somebody would be with us within the next few hours. I explained to Pete what was happening, made sure he was comfortable then settled onto the sofa to wait, thankfully, I didn't fall asleep and actually the carer was here sooner than expected.

It was thankfully someone who knew Pete and had worked with him before, which made it a little easier for me to go to bed and leave him, Pete was sleeping, relaxed by whatever he had drunk earlier.

Due to the condition of Pete's left hand, he could no longer straighten out his hand without the help of massage or foam rollers to grip. His wedding ring was becoming increasingly tighter and sadly needed to be taken off whilst we still could.

Pete came up with the ingenious suggestion of having a heart, drawn by me tattooed in place of his ring, have you ever tried drawing a heart on someone else's finger, it certainly created an interesting half-hour, much laughter and frustration until Pete was finally happy with my attempts and a heart shape he was happy with.

His mate Paul was going to do the tattoo (he was a registered tattooist), as well as putting no bad days across Pete's hand (lyrics of a song by Tom Odell, Liv introduced his music to us and the three of us had seen him in concert a few times), with a string of hearts leading down to the heart on his ring finger.

It looked amazing, very emotional, not the same as seeing the ring on his finger but a very good substitute.

Pete's hoist was no longer serving the purpose intended, apart from his hand he had no mobility whatsoever and it was becoming increasingly difficult to get him into his wheelchair with the H-hoist, a ceiling hoist was suggested, it would give us more freedom for transferring Pete (and stop the moving around of his riser/recliner).

A surveyor was arranged to come out and assess our ceiling to make sure it could take the weight, according to him all was good and a date was arranged for the removal of one hoist and fixing of the other.

On the day, the H-hoist was quickly removed, the workman looked around and said the new hoist wasn't suitable. Shit, they said a wall-mounted ceiling hoist would work, not as much freedom as the intended one but better than the H one, but they needed authorisation before they could do anything and thankfully, they did have one back at their depot in Winchester.

A heart-stopping few hours as we waited and time ticked by, literally minutes before they were going to leave (and leave us with no hoist whatsoever) the call came in giving them the go-ahead, bless them off they trotted and thankfully by the end of the day we had a working (weird-looking) wall-mounted ceiling hoist and the best thing ever. Pete could be hoisted onto the sofa and we could have a cuddle, priceless.

I had a check-in call with Southampton on Tuesday, for some reason, they didn't have my blood results and were a little concerned about me still feeling nauseous, although the Dr did say one of the antibiotics I'm on could be causing this and he'd check in with me again in two weeks by which time the nausea should be better and, of course, there'll be the obligatory blood tests to have before the call.

Yesterday, I had a check with Dr Noel, he didn't seem surprised about my nausea and he had my blood results, which are all good, in fact, I'm now in remission. That's the best news I've had in a while and I'm over the moon. There is a relatively new medication that if I take it, could keep me in remission for the next five years.

Obviously, I'll need to read up on the side effects and make my own mind up, but exciting news.

I still need to recover from the transplant, and my immunity levels are on the rise but very slowly. I should be able to have my COVID booster in January and my childhood immunisations in about a year.

I have to be very careful not to be near anybody with a cold, never mind anything else at the moment, but it'll be worth it in a few months when life will normalise again. My get-up-and-go, which has definitely gone at the moment, will return and I look forward to being able to get out and about and also being able to hug people again.

I am so happy, everything me and my body have been through over the last year and a bit has been worth it and I have a positive outcome. I'm officially in remission.

With Christmas fast approaching both our social calendars seemed never-ending, which is great as it gave us a bit of normality. Pete's running harem was due round for a takeaway.

Christmas meal out for me with my girlfriends, cousins coming for a visit, lunchtime drinks with the boys (Pete's mates), family visiting, that was as well as the clinic visits, therapist coming to the house to give Pete a foot massage (it was easier for him here than at the hospice).

Christmas Day, a meal was booked at a hotel about half an hour's drive away, we were going with friends. Phil was driving, Liv was with us and the carer had declined the offer of joining us. We were placed right at the back of the room as there were so many tables crammed into the room.

Pete was still eating small amounts of food, I just had to make sure it was cut up small enough and then feed him, great company, lovely meal but as soon as we'd eaten, Pete wanted to come home, he got uncomfortable if he spent too long in the chair (we were waiting for a new wheelchair cushion that would hopefully solve this problem).

So, we left our friends there and went home, at least, we had made it out, which in itself was an achievement.

Our family (kids and grandkids) Christmas was a few days after, as always, when they are around there is much laughter and sibling rivalry. Pete is never treated any differently, even by the grandkids (hard as it is for them).

Annabelle loves to help Pete eat, especially if chocolate or sweets are involved, it is usually two for her and one for Grampsy. Pete finds it hilarious, it's so good to hear the laughter, especially his when the kids are here, it always lifts his mood and mine for that matter. A day of fun, laughter, games, cheating, squabbling, food and much love, fantastic.

Our normal live-in career had the Christmas holidays off, I had got to use to him being around, knowing Pete, his needs and his routine it was a bit of a shock having different carers with us. I had to go through everything with them, routine, meds, how to feed him, and everything to do with his feeding tube, it made Pete very unsettled.

To be totally reliant on a stranger(s) (with my help) was so scary for him, something I'd never be able to understand and having different people living in our home, thankfully the normal carer came back and we both breathed a sigh of relief. Some carers are worth their weight in gold.

Although my cancer is in remission (it will never go away) I am monitored very closely. I have to have a bone marrow biopsy and blood tests to check everything is doing what it should be. I have also decided to give the tablets a go, if it prolongs my remission time it'll be worth it.

My get-up-and-go is finally coming back. I have to pace myself as Pete's second carer I still have to help and he prefers me to do certain things for him and, of course, just to keep him company.

I do still get very tired, and my mobility isn't great (especially my knees for some reason, they are so painful and I struggle to bend them without pain, my consultant is treating me for gout).

There is nothing worse than going for a nap and the carer tapping on my door as he needs help with Pete (usually being hoisted onto the commode), or I'm out for a walk and have to come back home as Pete needs the loo. All small things but have a big impact on my recovery, would I change it or have it any other way, definitely not.

Our social lives are very busy at the moment. I'm off for an annual girlie weekend away, this time to the Isle of Wight, where there will be much fun, laughter, drink and hugs (I don't drink, but it doesn't stop me from having fun), people will be dropping in on Pete whilst I'm away so I have no worries, he'll be off to the pub anyway.

Pete is still happy to go to town, usually driven by Macca when he goes, I chill for a few hours, if he is going to the local pub I go with him and drive (he struggles to take himself there), often meeting friends or having lunch. Pete is still eating, not lots but still able to enjoy what he can eat.

(He does have drink supplements to put into his rig if he doesn't feel like eating, so far he has refused them).

Friends come to visit, family comes by, and Pete's mum comes and spends a day with us every week. I can't begin to imagine how hard it is for her. Some friends and family struggle to see Pete as he is now and don't visit very often. I get that, but inside, he is still the same person, his body is failing him, not his mind. I know it upsets him even though he never says anything.

Pete is starting to choke more and more on his food which means changing the consistency of his food and sadly what he was able to actually eat, so far we've been able to clear the food, but it isn't nice to watch or see the look on Pete's face.

We had to call 999 for an ambulance as he choked on his saliva, thankfully Cheryl was with me, it was the look of fear in Pete's eyes as we struggled to help him. Thankfully, we stayed calm (goodness knows how) which gave him the reassurance he needed.

The ambulance was here in minutes, there wasn't a lot they could do, but helped calm Pete which brought his breathing under control and they got rid of the excess saliva which was causing the choking. On the surface, I was fine but I'd never been so scared.

I couldn't show Pete that, Cheryl was much the same, bless her. The career stood and watched us (our carer was on his break) and then declared she needed some training on choking!

I'd been taking the new medication for a number of weeks and felt worse than when I'd been having chemo, it was playing havoc with my guts (Colitis causes me issues now and again, the meds were aggravating it in my opinion) the pain and discomfort was unbearable.

Thankfully, I was due a phone check-up with my consultant, he prescribed some higher dose stuff to help with the cramping and decided to take me off the new medication for a month and then try a lower dose of it. Sad to say, even on the lower dose, my guts couldn't cope and it was decided to take me off of the medication, fingers crossed, I'm still going to be in remission for many years!

A Zoom call was arranged with CHC (Continuing Health Care), they funded Pete's health care package and needed to check Pete's continuing eligibility. I didn't like Zoom calls at the best of times, never mind doing anything like this.

Pete also needed to be included in the call and they wanted a lot of information which would be provided by our care agency and the hospice team, both thankfully would be on the call. I don't think I've ever been on anything so degrading, we had to sit and listen to everything Pete was or wasn't able to do, and then it was scored.

Pete was in tears (never good as he struggles to breathe when he gets upset), I was in tears, we went off the call, a discussion was done, and his score would determine if he could still have the funding. Very scary and thankfully, we were able to continue having the funding, plus a little more for double-up visits to try and take the pressure off me.

(I'm very much aware of how fortunate we were as so many people struggled to get what we had).

Even though it was really cold, we decided it would be a good idea to go for a beach day. Phil drove, Cheryl and grandkids followed in her car. Liv, carer, me and Pete in the van, off to Bournemouth we went. Flipping heck, it really was cold (bearing in mind, my hair was just thinking about regrowing).

I had a hat, scarf, thick jumper, and a big coat and still felt cold. Pete, on the other hand, didn't seem to feel the cold, he was wrapped up warmly, tucked in with a blanket and was quite happy. What I wasn't expecting was a strong feeling of emotions being back in Bournemouth (it was our favourite place).

The last time we were here was for a weekend away, just before I started my chemo and before Pete's MND diagnosis (it seemed like a lifetime ago).

I turned my head away so no one could see the tears welling up, brushed them away, said the wind was making my eyes water and stopped looking at the hotel we'd stayed in. Pete started turning his wheelchair in circles.

"Do you need some help?" I asked.

"No," he replied. "I'm fine, just a little cold."

We went to the restaurant on the pier, had fish and chips, Pete even managed to eat some, then went for a little walk, photos were taken for the carer who had never been to the beach before. Ice creams for those brave enough to eat them in the cold weather and then Pete was turning in circles again, he was getting cross so we decided to go back to the van and head for home.

I'm rubbish at walking and steering the wheelchair, so rather than antagonise Pete, Cheryl steered him back to the van, turns out he wasn't just cold, I found out on the way home he was struggling to control the wheelchair! A cold, lovely blustery day out and memories made.

Pete's mobility was continuing to decrease, not there was much more to lose mobility of, he could just about move his left hand and could still move his head and neck quite well. If we wanted or needed a hug, it was a case of me laying my head on his chest, putting my arms around him and Pete putting his head on mine, not great but better than nothing.

Wheelchair services came out and tried a different hand control for him, he couldn't get on with it, so I swapped back to the original one and had a conversation with wheelchair services, apparently there was a head control head rest they could try, but would need to order it and I asked if they could put a carer control on the back of the chair so we could control it if Pete couldn't.

Trying to get Pete into the house was both trying and hilarious, our hallway wasn't wide enough to walk bedside Pete and control the chair, it had to be done walking backwards, facing Pete and his chair.

The control was very sensitive and the slightest movement sent it into whatever direction had been pushed. I ran myself over many a time or sent the chair crashing into the wall causing Pete and myself to erupt into fits of laughter which in turn made it even harder to control the chair. (It was bad enough when moving the chair into position ready for him to be hoisted into or out of it, I even managed to run the carer over, luckily only once.)

The grandkids had asked for a sleepover, we often had them before COVID and our illnesses. Cheryl was going to stay too as we couldn't predict what sort of night Pete would have, or how many times I'd need to get up to help the night carer.

It gave a much-needed bit of normality to our very topsy turvy lives, the kids loved it. Pete loved it, it was noisy, chaotic, fun and great to wake up to having the kids in the house in the morning.

It was hard for them as well as they got to see what Grampsy's night routine was and the fact they couldn't come downstairs in the morning until he was up and in his chair, we so loved it.

Wheelchair services came to fit the new head rest, not before time as Pete hadn't been out and about much, it wasn't as easy to walk next to him to control his chair and he struggled to do it himself.

They also fitted the control at the back of the chair, so anyone could now help move it. Pete had his freedom back again, the smile on his face said it all. There were a few teething problems, we had to call wheelchair services back a few times but they were great, everything eventually got sorted and it was so much easier to walk and move Pete if needed with the new controller at the back of the chair.

Our regular live-in carer was due to go on a course, said when he would be back and stand-in carers arranged, I knew it would increase my workload and affect Pete's confidence with different people being around him. Thankfully, we now had the same regular night carers, who knew Pete quite well, knew his needs, knew how to work the CPAP and could understand him even though he had no speech.

It was about looking at his eyes when he needed something, once for yes, twice for no. I had also made crib sheets of things that made him uncomfortable at night, sometimes it worked, sometimes it didn't and it took ages for us to settle him.

I would never go to bed until I knew he was comfortable, no matter how long it took and I would kiss him goodnight when he was happy. This made things so much easier with different day carers as the night carers were able to show the day/night routines and take the pressure off me.

I watched over Pete with new carers, I was his eyes and ears, if I didn't like something or Pete was agitated, I stepped in. I called the care agency a few times with one of the new live-in carers. I wasn't happy on how Pete was being handled and asked if he'd had manual handling training.

Pete got so distressed at one point, I asked him to step away from him and I finished doing what Pete needed doing. I called the agency and asked for the person to be removed. I didn't trust him to look after Pete and Pete wasn't happy either.

I told the carer what I had done, he packed his bag and left, leaving me with no one for Pete, the care agency sent a day carer in (who did know Pete) to cover for a few hours whilst something was sorted.

Cheryl and Phil also arrived after I had told them what was happening, many phone calls later, someone was due to us later that evening, maybe! CHCs answer, if no one turns up and you can't cope, call 999, get him taken to hospital, after Pete's last experience that was the last thing I would be doing.

I called the hospice, they said to keep them informed, there was a possibility Pete could be admitted for respite care, if there was a bed available, so stressful for us, at least the night carer would be there as normal. Around 8 pm there was a knock at the door, a new live-in carer had thankfully arrived.

More phone calls followed the next day, the care agency we were with was going to be changed, they could no longer meet Pete's needs. I did ask if we could keep the night carers as that was working well and Pete felt confident in their hands.

Thankfully, CHC agreed to that, a new agency was found, a meeting arranged before handing over Pete's care, at the meeting, I checked the level of training the live-in carer would have, had they worked with MND people before, did they have manual handling and hoist training, had they used a

CPAP machine and did they know how to feed someone, yes was the answer given…Hmm!

Sadly, apart from manual handling and hoist training nothing else was true. I arranged for someone from the repository clinic to give a training session via Zoom to as many staff as they could spare, the training took place in our kitchen, three people turned up. I guess that's better than none.

I showed carers how to prepare Pete's food and how to feed him. I didn't want any more choking episodes, especially as he could now choke on his drinks as well as his food. How to position the CPAP mask and gently move it if it leaked (that sent the alarm off) and most importantly be gentle when handling Pete as he seemed to be getting a lot of pain, which I believe wasn't normal for MND suffers.

The live-in carers were turned around quite regularly, harder work for me, some got on with Pete some didn't, he was very quick to stand up for me if he thought what they asked of me was too much and told them off via his eye gaze, it amused me to watch the shock on their faces.

It certainly wasn't helping my recovery, but as far as I was concerned, Pete came first. Hopefully soon, we would get someone who would be with us for longer. In the meantime, Pete didn't like being left for too long and I never left him for longer than I needed to, even when going for blood tests and treatment.

(Even though I was in remission I was still having bone-strengthening infusions.) If friends were with Pete, I knew it was okay to be out and if the harem were there, I would usually go to Donna's, they would message me when they were leaving and I'd be home in a few minutes.

A fundraising evening was arranged (some members of the running club were running the London marathon for MND), it happened to be very near Pete's birthday, whoever needs an excuse for a party! Our kids, grandkids and friends turned up to support the evening, laughter, drink, many photos, especially with Pete and his harem.

I felt quite emotional, how many more evenings like this would there be, looking at Pete a big smile on his face, so happy, hopefully lots more, looking at his body and the struggle to actually get him there, probably not.

We were up the pub for Pete's birthday, he already had a birthday cake but a friend made him a cake in the shape of a gingerbread man, including orange hair (Pete referred to himself as strawberry blonde), we did laugh and the cake was delicious. Good friends are priceless.

A run/walk of 5K was taking place, again raising money towards the MND London marathon places, there was no set day, just proof you had completed it, paid your money and those taking part got a medal with Pete's photo on (nice touch).

I signed up to take part along with a group of friends, we were going to walk from local pub to pub, have a drink then walk back again, making it easier for me to actually complete the walk, very proud of myself. I did it and have the medal to prove it.

Our nephew Shaun was going to run from his home in Wales to our local pub, around 100 miles in distance over 24 hours raising money for MND, his brother Luke was going to ride alongside him and be supported by family and friends along the way. What an epic thing to do (the five km walk was more than enough for me).

A lot of people waited at the pub, us, other family members, friends and some of Pete's running club, some people went out to meet the boys and run the last leg with them. Pete was waiting at the finish, he was the first person they went to.

I stood back, watching, looking, such an emotional moment, so humbling. Very proud of them and the money raised for a worthwhile cause (if only they could find a cure or something to slow it down).

As I slowly get stronger, Pete is getting weaker, he is waking at night crying with pain and is very grumpy (as I guess anyone in pain would be) and I am making more calls to the hospice hub for help and advice for him.

A new cushion has been ordered for his wheelchair and for his riser recliner to try to ease the pain he feels around his bottom, we have cushions to put under his arms to ease the pain in his shoulders, ice packs to put wherever he needs them whenever he needs them, pain medication has been changed and increased as and when he needs it.

This has now prompted Pete to send me what he wants at his funeral, this caused many tears, mainly on my part as it is not something I really wanted to face, but I guess I'd rather know what Pete wanted, we know what the outcome is going to be and there is no point hiding from it.

We did have a discussion about going to Switzerland a few months after Pete's diagnosis, of assisted death, thankfully, when I read up about it he wouldn't have fitted the criteria, the only positive thing I think for MND. I'm glad he moved away from the idea.

In my opinion, it would have been worse than watching him slowly slip away from me, but at least we've had the opportunity to make memories, talk, laugh, sort things out and most importantly time together. The info Pete sent to me for his funeral wishes has been safely stored away, not for use just yet and besides that he keeps adding to it.

For the time being Pete is still happy, going out and about, socialising and for those that want to come visit him either at home or in the pub to come. We were up at the pub with friends, the carer took Pete out to the van whilst I picked his stuff up, noticed the glass door to the pub was smashed as I walked out but didn't think anything of it, got to the van and Pete was laughing, shoulders shaking, he didn't have the eye gaze so couldn't tell me what was causing him so much amusement.

When we got home, turns out he was the one who smashed the glass in the door at the pub, he had offered to pay for the door but the landlord said no, he thought it was really funny. I could see why he thought it was funny, all I could think of was what was the carer doing whilst he smashed into the door!

I seem to have lost my happy lovely Pete, he has been replaced by a very grumpy, pain-ridden, irritable replica, nothing I do is right, or good enough and he is rude to me. He accused me of forgetting to turn on the CPAP machine one night as it wasn't working properly.

I know I have chemo brain, but I'm not that forgetful, turns out the machine was misbehaving. Phil took it down to Southampton for us and picked up a replacement, it's a good job we have a spare (one for use and one for backup).

Pete is struggling at night, I'm woken most nights by his cries of pain or woken by the night carer as they can't understand what he wants, he is suffering from pain in his hamstring quite a lot, and the base of his spine or his arms, then there is the positioning in the bed, if he's placed too far down the mattress, he slips down the bed and his feet end up touching the end, again causing him pain.

Add in the CPAP constantly alarming, sometimes the carer can sort it sometimes they can't and I get up to reposition the mask, sometimes it works, sometimes I have to get up again to re-do it. I feel constantly worn out; the kids are worried I'm not getting enough sleep.

I daren't nap in the day as Pete is worried about being left alone with the carer, to be fair I'm not surprised, I've caught him on his phone as he's feeding Pete and on his phone when he was shaving Pete, thankfully, it was an electric razor! I was in the garden, the carer came out, sat down and went on his phone, stupidly I didn't send him in, Pete had been calling for him.

I spoke to the carer about the use of his phone, Pete's safety was first and foremost, the carer didn't like it and sulked, and the atmosphere was unbearable (it was like living with a sulky child, that's the carer not Pete).

If Pete wasn't positioned correctly on either the bed or in his chair, he seemed to slip down and become uncomfortable or the sling wrinkled up, it was a constant battle to reposition him to try and keep him comfortable or wriggling the sling down, which then pulled him down the bed or chair. No wonder we were all worn out.

There was also an issue with the positioning of the wee bottle for some reason the carers couldn't get it placed correctly causing wee to be spilt, usually over Pete.

This happened during the day, even when Pete had just got up (thankfully never at night) and obviously meant he needed clean dry clothes, more hoisting and messing around for him, was so frustrating. Sadly, at this point both of us struggled to find let alone keep our sense of humour.

I spent many a night crying into my pillow or hiding in the loo and shedding a few tears, my body hurt from moving Pete around and I was exhausted. I'm ashamed to say I did think how much easier it would be if he was no longer here, out of pain and no longer suffering, it was short-lived but still there.

I so needed a big cuddle, the person I wanted it from most was Pete. Occasionally, if I felt Pete was okay I would nip around to Donna's for a hug and time out, or I'd shut myself in my room and chat to family or friends. If I was still in the house, it wasn't unusual for Pete to call me down or send the carer up to get me, sometimes I just needed a little time out.

On top of everything else, Pete was struggling more with his food, he had another choking incident, which is why it's so important for everyone to pay attention when feeding him. Pete had so little confidence in people feeding him that I ended up doing it most of the time, but then I got it wrong at times as well, he had a Cornish pasty, so I thought I'd cut it lengthways to make it easier to eat.

Oh my goodness, you'd have thought I'd have committed a major crime, he ranted at me (amazing what he can put on the eye gaze), and said I was taking away his independence. I really had to grovel in my apology before he finally ate the thing, by this point, I felt like throwing it on the floor and having a temper tantrum (I didn't), all because I was trying to make things easier for him!

The dietician came to see Pete and gave him some different flavoured food supplements to try, at least, if he didn't feel like eating he could have these and they could go through his rig. He really struggled to swallow his medication so alternatives in liquid form were now needed, again these would be able to go through his rig.

Pete also removed people from Facebook and took himself off of his family group chat, he was struggling (thankfully not with just me), he was upset and he was frustrated at people he loved not coming to see him.

I know it's hard for people to see Pete this way, he just wants to be treated like he's normal. Very thankful for those who do spend time with him, no matter how hard it is for them and for our kids and grandkids.

No matter how crap he is feeling his mood always lifts when they are around, and he listens when they tell him off, especially when he's not nice to me. I know he doesn't mean it but it still doesn't make it easy for me.

Pete seems to be in constant pain again, this time, it's in his ribs, says it feels like he's broken a rib, as well as his bum and arms. Another call to the hospice, they suggested the physio come out to see him, also to show the carer how to do some of the exercises that hopefully will help ease his pain and the suggestion of using deep heat to alternate with the ice packs.

I'll happily give anything a go if it helps ease Pete's pain. The physio thankfully was able to fit Pete in very quickly, we got him comfortably on the bed and she set to work, showing the carer what she was doing as she went, I know Pete was in pain but hopefully, it would ease for a while at least.

The physio went and Pete wanted to stay on the bed, he was very chilled out, so the carer went over to him and started prodding him, saying, "Does this hurt?"

As he did it, FFS, what is the matter with the man, I'm sure he has no empathy. Thankfully, a different live-in carer is due any day, true to form the care agency is rubbish at communicating with us and we are reliant on being told what is happening by the carers (yes, I call the agency, and someone is always getting back to me, I choose my battles).

Pete did sleep better and he woke in a much better mood, my Pete is back, even managed to laugh together when I told him off for getting grumpy, there is a sadness in his eyes that breaks my heart and he has told me more than once over the last few days that he has had enough.

I've also noticed he is choosing not to use his CPAP as much during the day, always at night, it still alarms and wakes me up, I listen to make sure the night carer sorts it, if not, I go downstairs. We have a new live-in carer, someone who actually listens to what we say, yes he did spill wee over Pete the first day (not a great start), but he put into practice our advice, mastered the medication and most importantly talked to Pete, listening to what he had to say.

I could see, Pete starting to relax around him, I felt confident enough to leave him on his own with the carer and Pete was happy with that. What a relief especially as I was off out to a friend's 60th party in a few days (a bit selfish of me, I know). Pete's friends were dropping around whilst I was out, so I knew they'd look after him.

All the kids and grandkids were over to celebrate Liv's birthday, Pete managed to eat some of the food but especially loved the cake as I put custard with it to make it easier for him to swallow, as always he's happier when they are around him, especially as they bring Cheryl's new puppy, she licks him to death, love it.

I noticed Pete's body was becoming more *slumpy*, as if his muscles were now giving up on him, this could be why he struggles to get comfortable and we struggle to get him in the right positions, especially when placing him in his wheelchair.

Although he has stopped people from visiting if he hasn't felt like having company and has not gone out when he should have on the whole he is still very sociable and does like going out but not for as long as he gets uncomfortable. Friends were holding a charity football match, raising funds for MND. Pete wanted to go, he even managed to stay for the whole match, he loved being the centre of attention and caught up with so many friends and family.

The therapy team decided to try Pete on a tilt-and-turn mattress, hopefully, it would mean the night carers wouldn't need to move Pete around to get him comfortable and he would get a better night's sleep. What I didn't anticipate was being handed a plastic bag of bits and pieces and being told the therapy team would know what to do with it, really, thankfully they did.

On the first night, he did get a better night's sleep, sadly the carer forgot to turn it off when they were getting him up, he actually face-planted the safety rail of his bed, he wasn't hurt and because I laughed, he laughed, lesson learnt for the carers, remember to switch it off before moving Pete in the mornings.

Even though Pete has no speech, it's amazing how looks and grunts can tell me off, or emphasise when he's cross with me (still too often for my liking), this is mainly at bedtime when he's tired anyway. We just can't seem to get his pain under control, if he has too much the pain relief it makes him drowsy, which he doesn't like.

I just don't know what the answer is. Some days, I hide away in the garden, trying to have a nap especially if Pete is napping (he does know I'm out there), sometimes he'll ask to join me outside, it takes longer to hoist him into the chair and get him comfortable than he's actually outside, at least, he gets some fresh air.

I felt like I had a cold or was it hay fever, either way, I felt rubbish. Pete, bless him, once he was comfortable in the chair tried not to fidget or move so he wouldn't need repositioning, he even said he wouldn't have a poo so I could rest, bless him he does make me laugh and how nice to see my lovely caring man is still there.

He actually needed two poos, and the night carer arrived so I was able to escape upstairs early, daren't give Pete his usual goodnight kiss as didn't want to share my germs.

It's now Pete's right arm that is causing him pain, pain relief and a warmed-up heating bag seem to ease it. Why, oh why, does he have all this pain? He then choked on a love heart sweet, yesterday, he'd eaten some and had been fine, but today not.

I had to yell for the stand-in carer to come help me, thank goodness, I knew what to do. Sadly, no more love hearts for him and to make things worse, his mum was round to see him choke.

To give himself something to do, Pete decided to hold a quiz night to raise money for MND, with the help of Macca and a few others he did it all (thank goodness for the eye gaze and emails) there were many prizes donated for raffle prizes, my help wasn't needed which was great. When we arrived at the venue there was hardly anywhere for us to go it was so busy.

I did manage to find a comer for us, got Pete settled, grabbed a few chairs for us, went to the van to bring in the raffle prizes, and then went to move the van and breathe. The night started with a speech written by Pete, read by the quiz master, the last part of it was an acknowledgement to me and everyone in the room raising a toast to me!

Both of us got a bit emotional. A great evening was had by all, well over £2000 raised, tired but happy Pete, was put to bed that night and I didn't hear a peep from him. I so love this man.

Pete got a message from friends sitting next to us, she'd tested positive for COVID that morning, shit.

Pete tested positive a few days later, I tried to avoid him but it was almost impossible, the live-in carer had changed over, thankfully, it's someone who's been before, so does knows Pete's routine.

He was due to have someone come out to give him the antiviral meds intravenously when they arrived they struggled to get a vein to put a line in him (Pete had struggled to give blood, so I wasn't surprised), bless them they tried everything except his groin area, they said that was too invasive, they had to leave without Pete having the drug and there was no way he could have it orally.

I informed the care agency so they could take the necessary precautions. I tested positive a few days later, a call to my consultant and antiviral meds were delivered that day for me, I stayed in my room and asked Liv if she could stay home for a few days to help out (she had COVID the week before, but not been home).

She struggled with Pete's grumpiness, he was feeling ill, and still had a lot of pain to contend with and I wasn't around. Whilst Liv was helping us, she sang for Pete and her boyfriend Tris played the guitar, so lovely to watch. I couldn't sit with them, so I sat on the stairs watching, listening and videoing them. Seeing the smile on Pete's face was priceless.

All therapy and social visits were cancelled, we were in isolation. I usually made Pete's meals so the carer didn't really know what to feed him (ask him), his appetite wasn't great anymore anyway, and then we ran out of wet wipes.

Pete messaged me the carer had used a towel and then left it in the chair! Pete found it easier to sleep in his chair, his body had become really sensitive due to COVID, and he said he slept like a baby. Even though I was taking the medication I felt really rough and didn't even have the energy or feel like sitting on the stairs to talk to Pete.

Cheryl came over, all masked up, I heard Pete crying, when she came up to see me I asked what she had done to Pete, she said he was just happy to see her. It took a few days but I started to feel better, just totally exhausted. Dr and nurse from the hospice came out to check on Pete, they were surprised at how well he was doing.

COVID seemed to have taken his pain away, for the time being anyway, they checked on his well-being, and did he still want to be here, he said definitely, he definitely had goals to keep, and he wanted to go watch some of his harem ladies run the London marathon, he just needed to memo his body to keep up with his mind, his meds were tweaked and they went away happy.

Much as I don't want to lose Pete, October seems such a long way away. I don't know if I want him here that long, seeing his pain, his deterioration, the sadness in his eyes is so hard, keeping on top of his medication, the carers, moving and handling him and the day-to-day stuff, it's tough.

I'm a strong person but I'm buckling, I'm exhausted. I know some of this is COVID talking but finally, we both tested negative on the same day, apart from tiredness for both of us we seem to have got off quite lightly without any lingering effects from COVID.

Things seem to have gone to pot with the carer since I've not been around, don't know what he's been doing, certainly not looking after Pete very well, forgetting Pete's meds, spilling wee on him, thankfully I'll be around more to keep an eye on him, it's probably a good job Pete's not been eating much, at least he can put a supplement down Pete's rig without too much bother.

On top of all the pain Pete is now getting pain in his heels, especially at night, elevating them with a cushion seems to help, the cushions we use for the pain in his arms during the day double up for his heels at night, resulting in more pain relief which is incorporated into his night routine.

Hopefully, that'll keep him settled. The night carer hadn't turned up, called the agency, and they called back, apparently, he'd fallen asleep and was on his way, live-in carer asked if I would help put Pete to bed as he needed to nip to the shop.

Pete was settled down quite quickly and I sat with him until the night carer arrived. The live-in carer was also having an issue with jobs he should be doing, I'd mentioned about Pete's shirts needing ironing, and he then asked if the relief carer could do the ironing.

I assumed the carers did the same jobs, but checked with the agency anyway, no idea what was said between the carers but the live-in carer ended up doing the ironing.

Pete had slid down in the chair, and needed shuffling up the chair, the carer refused to move Pete unless I helped him.

I physically struggle to move Pete's body weight, it hurts me so much but there's no way I'd see Pete uncomfortable. Usually, I hold onto the sling to stop it from moving, the carer shuffles Pete to one side then we swap sides and repeat, no, I had to move him, it hurt and pissed me off.

Pete knew I shouldn't be doing it and was mad, when he was settled he had words (via the eye gaze) with the carer, he wasn't happy, in fact, none of us were, awkward.

Liv and Tris went back to London today, the house is strangely quiet.

The alarm on the CPAP seems to be going off a lot during the night. I don't know why.

Phil came over and made breakfast, so glad as I was exhausted. Cheryl and the kids came over for lunch, busy and chaotic, lovely then calm. I was tired so slept for a bit in the garden, the antidepressant increase is working as Pete is definitely calmer, and more relaxed, but sadly, it hasn't helped his pain which is kicking in more and more.

Scarily, Pete said he wanted to transfer some savings over to me, just in case! In case of what, I didn't want to ask, considering a few days before he'd wanted to be here in October, had he read my mind!

Pete is quiet at the moment, he has been coughing a lot every time he eats or drinks and he says his tummy is sore, he had two poos and then needed to go again. I got a little cross so he said he wouldn't go as I was angry. I told him not to be so silly, it's more the fact I seem to be doing most of the work, when I said something to the carer he said he was protecting his back.

When Pete was settled back in the chair, he said something to the carer (via eye gaze), that I didn't hear as I was on the phone with Liv. He said he wanted to sleep in the chair tonight, he does seem to sleep better, shame it doesn't always ease his pain.

He told me he's chosen a car for me (I reckon it because I told him I'd be quite happy with a Kia of some sort when I have to trade in the van), a Qashqai, hmm, Pete is a bit of a car snob, we'll see when the time comes.

He also told me about his pensions (not that I didn't know about them) and mentioned about transferring money around, now I'm getting a little scared.

I have been wetting Pete's mouth with a sponge, it seems to help him grip the straw when he drinks, not sure if it's due to all the meds he is on, the speech and language lady came out today. Pete's swallow has deteriorated, which means his food has to be soft and mushy, or just small tastes of food and uses his food supplements if he doesn't want to eat, very hard for someone who loves their food.

Drinks now need to be one sip at a time, fluid can be and is often put through his rig to keep him hydrated, he is struggling more to actually sip from a straw, and doesn't seem to have the strength. It really brings it home how much the onslaught continues internally to his body, stuff we can't see.

A member of the therapy team was out to try a neck brace on Pete, he was adamant he didn't want it, to be fair he doesn't need it at the moment but it is a lot smaller and unobtrusive than he thought, so it was left with us.

It is also thought Pete might be bunged up, which is causing the pain in his tummy, so he's taking laxatives to see if it helps. (The amount he poops I don't think so but then I'm not a medical professional).

I was having an evening out with my sister, and Phil was coming over to keep Pete company before he arrived Pete messaged me and said the carer had asked if he could go out for half an hour, leaving Pete on his own, obviously, he didn't.

What is the matter with some of these carers, do they have no common sense? After a rubbish few days, Pete had a visit from Andy, he hadn't been round in a while so it really cheered him up.

Pete did say, he thought his time was nearing but he wasn't ready to go to the hospice yet, we'd had a conversation about where he wanted to die, and I'd said I would struggle (selfishly) if he was home as we'd not lived in the house long enough to make memories (we'd been in the house about 15 months) and I didn't know if I'd be able to carry on living here.

I know it's inevitable and we've had lots of very frank conversations about his death, but it's the first time Pete's mentioned he felt he was nearing the end, I don't like it and I did shed a few tears.

I've learnt with initial difficulty to take Pete's contact lenses in/out, it's not easy, sometimes it takes me ages to put them in (I start laughing for some reason), and other times, they go straight in, luckily, I've not lost any, just dropped them and had to replace them.

I've noticed he has been wearing his glasses more than the contacts lately, hopefully, it's just because he got fed up with the amount of time it takes for me to put them in and not because they're causing issues with his eyes. We did try to get an eye appointment but they couldn't accommodate his wheelchair and home appointments don't cover contact lenses, so his eyes need to stay healthy.

Had a much-needed few hours up the pub with Donna, then joined by Liv and Phil, so good to be out and feeling normal, although Pete had said it was fine, he was very crabby when I got home and for the rest of the evening, didn't want any tea, not sure if he was punishing me for being out, very hard to tell these days.

Happy 21st anniversary to us. Pete isn't going out much at the moment so very low-key celebrations, beautiful bouquets of flowers from Pete. He's got curry for tea, hopefully, he'll be able to eat it, strange some days he can manage food relatively well, others he can't or doesn't want it. In so much pain today.

I sit and massage his right hand, then put the heated wheat bag on his arm before massaging the other hand, which seems to ease his arm pain, cushion under his heels, and comfy Pete for a while at least. He ate the curry and had ice cream as well, and fell asleep waiting to go to bed. He is a lot more sleepy, I guess from so much medication.

Pete couldn't eat the fresh sausage roll today, so I did a stupid thing, it had onion in and gave me stomach cramps to the point of having to lie-down, that'll teach me. Interesting chat with Pete about the future without him, said he'd haunt me if I got another man. I asked him what if I wanted a companion, and he said he didn't want anyone taking his money.

I said that would never happen, the kids would make sure of that (and probably scare any men away), and we were laughing. He then said he needed to stop fighting, if his time was up, it was up, his mind might be wanting to live as long as possible, but sadly his body is not, COVID has certainly taken its toll. Andy and Macca were due to come around, but Pete cancelled them, he wasn't up to it.

Pete has voiced the words I have been dreading, "I've had enough."

I'm not totally surprised, I've seen it in his eyes over the last week or so, he just wants to be made comfortable. It made me cry, he is in so much pain, he can see I'm struggling and he knows he'll only get worse. I knew this was coming but it doesn't make it any easier when Pete has actually voiced it.

I phoned the hospice for advice and was told to up his morphine patch and give him oral morphine every three hours if needed, this may help his pain but will make him more drowsy and poop more. It's really whatever makes him more comfortable.

Pete hasn't left the house in four weeks, he's grumpy, tired a lot of the time and agitated, not just with me, but with both day and night carers. He seems to be struggling with his eye gaze as well, which in turn means, he's not able to communicate his needs as easily and which then frustrates him even more.

He has also decided to stop taking one of his meds as he feels it's not helping him, checked with the hospice it was okay to do this and he voiced about stopping the use of his CPAP, I said he would need to wait till the doctor came before doing that.

I'd been out for a bit, and come back, Pete said he needed a wee, then changed it to say he needed a poop and he had just farted and possibly followed through, what do you say to that, nothing at all except clean him up, hoist him and sit him on the commode.

Whilst he's sat there, I clean and disinfect the chair, and check his shorts out. I'm tempted to chuck them out but they're designer ones so soak them before giving them a good scrub.

All clean and sorted, then we sat Pete on a towel in his chair and covered him with another towel to protect his modesty, it's too early for bed but Pete didn't want bed shorts or shorts on, just in case!

Spray the room liberally with air freshener, no one would ever know. When you love someone you'll do anything for them.

I would love to *just* be Pete's wife for a little while, being his lover has long since gone, and even being his friend seems impossible these days. MND has just taken him over, It's hard when I'm tired, frustrated, in pain and just want a bit of normality in our lives.

I often don't have time to eat or forget or I'm too tired. I did try to find a respite place we could go, so we could be *normal* even for a few days but I couldn't find anything nearby.

My sense of humour has slipped a little and Pete's has all but disappeared, still, if I can make him at least smile every day (believe me that's not hard with my chemo brain and the things that I say) I'm happy. In my opinion, laughter is the best medicine.

Pete's night times are becoming increasingly unsettled, the night carers are good but it's the lack of understanding of what Pete needs (which changes often by the minute) and the frustration at not being able to make himself understood, which then makes him agitated. I sleep with a listening ear.

I'll leave the carer to try to settle Pete before going down to help, or the carer will come get me. Sometimes, it can be the simplest of things, his pillow isn't right, his mouth is dry and needs wetting, pain is sometimes harder to sort, ice/heat/pain relief will usually get it under control, shuffling him up the bed seems harder at night but it's still doable, even if it means hoisting him up to reposition him, or repositioning the CPAP mask.

On one particular night, we were struggling to settle Pete as he went to bed, I went through everything I could think it might be, nope, he was cross and agitated. I was cross, and the carers were frustrated.

I repositioned his pillow that had slipped, he smiled at me, it had been the pillow that was the issue, the thing I'd mentioned at the beginning, he was obviously so cross he hadn't heard, it's usually the simple things, finally settled, off to bed I went, actually chuckling to myself.

The worst and most scary thing is, if he chokes in bed, it's so much harder to sit him upright, quickly, whilst calming him and trying to get his breathing under control, thankfully it only happened once, scared the shit out of me, Pete and the carer. It would be interesting to be a fly on the wall at night, listening to our exchanges!

Pete loves it when friends and family come by. Macca if not at the pub with him comes round for a cuppa. Andy pops in, some or all of the Harem ladies visit regularly. Cheryl visits regularly, with Jay and with the kids, as I've mentioned before the grandkids just see their Grampsy, not the MND (love kids and their ability to take things in their stride).

Liv comes home as often as she can, to be fair she is coping far better than I thought she would, her dad is her world and I always call Phil if there is a technical issue, not that he doesn't come over anyway. I know this helps Pete to feel normal, but it saddens him that (and me) people struggle to see past his failing body to the person and mind that is still so with us.

So excited to have reflexology at the hospice today, my piece of light relief and normality, the carer Pete likes and trusts is back, so I know, he'll be fine for a while. I managed to speak to the doctor whilst there and explained that Pete had had enough, didn't want to use his CPAP anymore, just wanted to be made comfortable and didn't want to die at home.

She did explain to me that it could still take a while for him to die, she'd come to the house to talk to him and sort things out. Very proud of myself, obviously had my big girl pants on and managed not to cry throughout the conversation.

True to her word, the doc came out later that day, had a very frank chat with Pete, told him not to expect things to happen quickly, and updated his purple form (end-of-life preferences). They would introduce meds to help keep him calm and he should be able to go to the hospice when the time was right, it seemed so surreal, like I was watching from the outside.

The night carer was prepared, and pain relief and calming meds were on the kitchen side, the first night without the CPAP, let's see what it brings.

Lots of coughing throughout the night, I went down at one point to see if he wanted the cough assist (helps him cough and clear his chest), made a cuppa and went back to bed, neither of us got much sleep, but we'd made it through the night.

Up early to drop the car off at the garage, yep, normal life still goes on. The door on the van is playing up, so need to get it sorted out. Doc called early to check on Pete, and then lovely nurses from the hospice arrived, all I can say is poor Pete, was attacked from all angles, first the pain driver, then a catheter (Doc hadn't mentioned that) and finally a suppository, fingers crossed this would sort his pooping out.

He sat on the loo for over two hours, hoisting has just got a little more complicated, the sling digs the catheter into his leg and we have to keep an eye on the tube from the pain driver, practice will make perfect.

There is also a bed ready at the hospice, and the doctor would prefer Pete to go in sooner rather than later, but he's not quite ready yet and they left a box of end-of-life medication, no idea what's in it and I don't want to know.

The kids know what is happening. I am now faced with the task of telling those Pete wants to know. He needed another poop, my goodness, the smell, was far worse than when he pooped himself. I'm gagging, made me feel quite ill, think it made Pete feel better and gave him a laugh at my reaction.

You know you think you've prepared yourself and it's gonna be okay, you'll be able to cope, that's just crap, it's as scary as hell when it actually happens. In a very sad way, it means, I'll finally get to be Pete's wife, not his carer when he's in the hospice.

Called the care agency to inform them of what was going on and to ask if we could have regular carers for however long

Pete had left, it would make him feel more comfortable and relaxed.

Pete had the best night's sleep in a long time but was still very sleepy when it was time to get up, guess this is what it'll be like going forward. He needed a poop just as the night carer was due to leave, bless them they stayed to help, first time in I can't remember I've not had to help.

Cheryl, grandkids and Phil came for lunch, put a smile on Pete's face and kept him awake for a while. The nurses came to sort his pain driver, chased his meds at the surgery for me and tweaked his pain relief as they could see he was still in pain.

Phil went to pick up meds for me (not the first time we'd had to chase medication and run around to get it, thankfully the chemist even got them right this time, the joys of having so much medication).

Cheryl called Macca and Andy to update them, I went to see Pete's mum and spent a bit of time with her after I had told her, then onto one sister, the other sister wasn't in, spoke to her via her doorbell, modem technology, then calls to his brothers, emotionally worn out, but it's done.

Pete's getting cross/frustrated with the eye gaze, I think the meds are affecting his ability to use it, tiredness is probably not letting him concentrate, crap that's his communication going down the pan.

Pete is coughing more in the night and takes a while to cough up whatever is troubling him, even with the cough assist, the doc was out to check on him with one of the nurses, and they gave him a jab (with his permission) which stopped him coughing immediately, he's still holding his own which is good.

His mum came over with one of his brothers and sister-in-law, they left his mum here for a few hours and his sister would pick her up later. Pete is still interested in food even though most days, he doesn't eat much, he's asked for a chilli today, think I should be able to make that without causing him to choke, fingers crossed.

Macca and Andy came around, asking lots of questions, sadly I couldn't answer them but good to see them. I ate one of Pete's cookies, he was livid, he wanted the kids to go buy him more, I had to laugh (without him seeing me), it's not like he can eat all of them.

Off to the beach, took a while to get Pete settled into the wheelchair, his body is very slumpy, guess muscle control is going, need to prop him up with a cushion, he even used the collar not so long ago we didn't think he would need.

Interestingly, he can no longer control the wheelchair, he doesn't have enough movement in his head. I wonder if that's why he stopped going out and all the frustration of trying to get him positioned properly, why is he so stubborn and proud?

Today is going to be fun. I'm still rubbish at steering the chair, I crash into everything and anything, oops. I'll let the carer do it. Pete can get cross at him rather than me. We're joined by the kids, a family day out to Southsea, the sun is shining, a lovely summer day.

Pete ate fish (very carefully given to him) we ate the chips followed by ice cream, funnily enough, Pete didn't need much help with that. We watched the hovercraft going in and out, Pete couldn't get to the water's edge but Cheryl got him a nice slippery bit of seaweed to go over his legs to make him feel part of it.

He did have a light blanket on to protect his legs from the sun and hide the catheter, he was cross about it but I'm always practical, so I won. He slept all the way home, very slumped to the left, not sure if that was partly due to Phil's driving!

He said his bucket list was now complete; he was ready to go. I went to check on him during the night, he was very warm, I wiped him down with a cool flannel, at least his breathing was better than the wheezing he'd gone to bed with.

I got a call from my consultant whilst we'd been at the beach, he was very pleased with my blood and was stopping all medication apart from calcium and vitamin D pills and bone-strengthening infusion, what a result no more medication, so pleased, it seems as my body continues to recover Pete's is sadly declining.

Saying that after our day at the beach, my body is aching, my vision is a bit blurry and I have a headache, hopefully, caused by the withdrawal of my meds, paracetamol and a nap will hopefully help.

Since Pete has stopped using the CPAP he has been coughing more, especially at night. I've been up and given him the cough assist, which does help, but doesn't clear the cough completely, he has lost his appetite, is struggling to sip through the straw and is becoming drowsier.

When the nurses come to do his meds, they up one of them to help with the coughing, but could lead to a dry mouth. Pete's happy to cope with that, although still in pain he doesn't want his meds increased as it'll make him even more drowsy.

He asked about my brother, sister and aunty visiting, funnily enough Ivan and Kim then arrived (brother and sister-in-law), and said I'd check when my sister and aunty were due to visit.

Pete does seem to like my chilli (made with lots of sauce), very easy for him to swallow, he had some for tea, asked for more, then accused me of huffing (I probably did) so refused to eat it. I didn't have the energy to argue with him, struggling with his coughing, and grunting noises, seems like he was going to go on and on.

I miss the person he should be and would love to have my man back and feel his strong arms around me, I don't even have the energy to cry. Didn't help two of his harems were here tonight, had to tell them, resulting in lots of tears.

Phil's taking me for my infusion today. Macca's popping in to see Pete and the live-in carer has said, he'll stay till the end of the week, thank goodness for that someone was supposed to come to shadow the carer, but they never showed up and they were trying to give us an inexperienced live-in carer for a replacement.

What is it with the care agencies that say they have the necessary people to care for Pete when actually they don't? It is so stressful, frightening and worrying for both of us, pretty shit really. In some ways, I hope Pete will be going into the hospice when our current carer goes on his break, so sad I'd even think like that, but it's the reality.

Nurse came in to see Pete, upped his pain meds, also offered him a jab to help with the pain, asked about his dry mouth, gave me some gel stuff with a sponge applicator and we talked about ways of helping him drink a teaspoon, syringe, sponge, then I asked what to expect as the days go on!

Sleepiness (that's already started), disinterest in his surroundings, not wanting to get up, thankfully none of those at the moment. I also asked if I'd be able to stay with Pete. Liv and Tris were scrambling around in the attic as we talked, life seemed to carry on as normal all around us and then his sister came to visit, she'd not been for a while as she struggled to see him as he was.

I went to the pub with a friend, hadn't seen her in a while, lovely to get out for a bit, especially as I was still not feeling great. I startled Pete as I came in, he'd been napping, relief carer had forgotten to give him any food whilst I was out.

FFS meant he was past wanting anything, not even a supplement. Pete spent most of the evening napping, waking to poop, then back to sleep, very strange having him too quiet, his breathing is becoming noisier and he has been struggling to breathe through his nose, have been trying Obis nose stuff which the carer gives him, that seems to help and he has started dribbling.

Cheryl and the kids come over, Lola (dog) has discovered she is now big enough to jump onto Pete's chair and cover him with licks. Annabelle painted Pete's finger and toenails rainbow colours, he loved it; to be fair there isn't a lot he can do to stop her.

The hospice nurse bought some memory boxes, Cheryl decided they were too big, we'd source our own ones, so she took them back with her. Pete asked the nurse if they had sky in the hospice, and she said she'd find out for him. At least, the meds in his pain driver are helping, we're not having to use the ice packs at the moment and he's not crying out in pain.

Bad night for Pete and he's not great this morning either, struggling with his breathing, the night carer never came to get me, they should've. I still don't sleep well, always listening out, it's even stranger now as there's no alarm going off, you'd think it would make it easier, but no it's harder, can't hear him coughing since he had that jab, so I have to listen harder.

Call from the hospice nurse, good news for Pete, not only do they have sky, but they also have sky sports and there is a bed available either today or tomorrow, crap, now it's real.

I called the kids, and both care agencies, the night agency called to check on us, but they didn't really know what to say. Kids and grandkids spend the day, with much laughter, fun and games, including wrapping Phil in cling film, so funny watching the girls trying to keep his hands still as the other wraps him.

Barb popped in for an hour, giving me much-needed moral support, always good to spend time with her. Takeaway curry for tea, Pete even managed some which was nice to see. Cheryl helped me pack a bag with some of Pete's stuff before they left for the night. I did have a few tears but on the whole, I thought I managed to keep it together very well.

I found out recently, what had made Pete cry all those weeks ago when we were getting over COVID. Cheryl was pregnant, very early stages, she'd told Pete as soon as she knew, but not me.

Pete chose a cuddly bunny and I found a football rattle (I wanted to get something from Arsenal but Pete refused, saying a child would always follow the dad's football team, sadly Jay supports Chelsea) and got a vest with *love from*

Grampsy on, put it all in a box and took a photo before Pete went into the hospice.

Talk about emotional, doing this knowing Pete will never get to meet the baby, but so glad they will always have something from him.

Typical, Pete had a good night and was in good spirits. I was up, showered, dressed and packed his stuff. Cheryl arrived, she was driving us, and the grandkids came to say goodbye, the decision had been made for them not to come to see Pete in the hospice, better for them to have memories in the house, everything was going fine until Joshua got upset, then Pete cried.

I had to put one of his pills under his tongue to calm him. I had to support his head on the journey he couldn't keep it up. The kids stayed at the house with Liv, we dropped the carer at the train station en route to the hospice, then it was a case of taking his stuff in, luckily, there was help on hand from the lovely staff.

A double bed was in Pete's room, somewhere for me to sleep, and a whiteboard for us to put all the info about family, friends, likes and dislikes, what an easy way for staff to get to know patients and there was somewhere for Pete to put photos and things he wanted to see on the wall in front of him.

All the eye gaze stuff Pete required was set up so he'd still be able to communicate, his stuff was all put away, and we were shown around, a family room, shower room for family members, kitchen area, shower/bathroom for patients, very calm atmosphere and Pete seemed so relaxed.

I left him in very capable hands and nipped home for a bit to drop Cheryl off and pick up the commode, we'll actually be able to use the downstairs loo and the posh toilet.

I spent the rest of the day with Pete, he does have sky but it won't work with Pete's eye gaze so he is reliant on others changing channels for him, fine as long as he has use of the eye gaze, at least I know he wants sky sports most of the time, just don't let me loose with the remote.

I've already cocked it up and had to get help, It was timing out, I pressed the wrong button, It timed off and couldn't get it back on again, oops. I didn't sleep over and didn't expect the onslaught of emotions when walking through the door and seeing Pete's empty chair, the house is eerily quiet even with Liv and Tris in it, no live-in carer, no hushed talking from the carer, all the preparing and it's still bloody hard.

The first morning after a restless night, on the way to see Pete, I decided to go to the Toyota garage and look at cars, a bit of a waste of time really. I couldn't stop crying and the man wasn't very helpful, maybe, next time, I need to take someone with me.

So many visitors come to see Pete and most leave their mark on Pete's information board causing much amusement amongst the staff, he also gets to have a shower, the first one in over a year, and he so enjoyed it. I can't begin to imagine what it must've felt like.

I slept over, the first time I've shared a room with Pete in over a year. I can just about squeeze myself onto his bed for a cuddle, even if I have one leg hanging off the bed, it's still a cuddle and causes us to both laugh. I get breakfast and lunch when I stay over, nothing is ever too much trouble for the staff and I hang out in the family room when Pete naps or needs a poop (there is always a supply of homemade cake or biscuits, yum!) or there are too many visitors to see him.

The harem came to visit, bringing wine (Pete gets to have a beer or wine of his choice in the evening), and much laughter and noise. Liv and Tris brought the guitar up, singing and playing for him one evening.

Donna came up to watch footie with us, it's all very sociable and lovely. I ask Cheryl if she's telling people about the pregnancy yet. Pete has a scan photo on his wall which is up and down like a yoyo as no one knows yet.

Phil, Cheryl, Jay, and Lola (pets were encouraged, one evening Lola was visiting, she loved all the attention, she came trotting around the corner, and made a nurse jump, causing her to shriek, scaring the living daylights out of everyone before we all ended crying tears of laughter).

Liv, Tris, Macca and Andy are constant visitors, other friends, work colleagues, past and present also visit (I thought Liv would struggle to come see him, but she has proved me wrong). If I don't sleep over, I leave usually as the night shift comes on, making sure Pete is settled.

This works quite well apart from Pete's struggle with communicating his needs, sometimes he can't make himself heard at night and on more than one occasion has messaged me asking to go back as he needs a poop, or is in pain, thankfully a call from me to the hospice hub has managed to get everything sorted.

It has resulted in a monitor being placed in Pete's room at night which is switched on and thankfully seems to have resolved the issues.

I was resting on a sleepover, listening to staff as they made Pete comfortable, there were three staff members, chatting to Pete as they worked, they switched the mattress on, saying it sounded noisy, then realised the pump hose wasn't attached, causing us all (including Pete) to laugh.

Pete tried to chat with staff as much as he could and would call them by their name via his eye gaze. I know they really appreciated it.

Pete's mum visits, and either his brother or one of his sisters drops her off, and then someone else will pick her up. His family from Wales visit when they can, and his sister brought our nephew and girlfriend for a visit, it caught Pete off guard and he wasn't happy, which resulted in him posting a message on the family chat that if people hadn't visited him in a while don't bother coming to see him now.

Oops, trust Pete, did result in a few snotty messages to me, seriously, like I don't have other things on my mind, families! Someone also asked if they could have a photo of Pete, no, I don't have any of his time in the hospice, why would I? It is so lovely to finally be Pete's wife again.

I feed Pete, not that he eats much, but everything else is done by the staff, they'd do his washing as well but it's just as easy for me to do it on my visits home, it's strange how quickly we've adapted to a new, different routine.

I'm home alone for the first time, I tidy, hoover, make phone calls and try to watch a film. I feel empty, scared, and frightened to cry, in case, I don't stop, everyone thinks I'm brave, and strong, at this moment I feel so lost and alone.

Pete's condition seems to have stabilised since coming to the hospice (not unusual for MND), which must be due to the fantastic care he is receiving, this gives a new dilemma.

Pete could be sent back home, he doesn't want it and in the nicest possible way, I don't want it either (one of the reasons, I haven't got rid of the van or any of his stuff at home, just in case), we have a meeting with his doctor, they are going to review him in a week's time.

Goodness knows what that means, there are no facilities, no homes for Pete to go to, and he would have to come back home, apart from sleeping a lot more everyone has said how well he looks!

Although it's great to spend more time with Pete, not having to care for him, the coming backwards and forwards is taking its toll, I can't sleep at home and don't sleep well if I stay. I'm tired and my body is hurting. I know his time is creeping nearer, even if he appears more stable at the moment.

Lots of visitors are tiring Pete, more family, more friends, lovely as it is to hear the laughter, he is struggling, he's starting to get more pain, in his ribs, his breathing is more noisy and grunting noises, he coughs more if he drinks or eats anything, his bum is sore (no bed sores) and he is now struggling with the eye gaze.

I'm struggling with his contacts, so wonder if his eyes are dry, which would make using the eye gaze harder. I have another sleepover, Pete is restless, I get used to his noisy breathing, and try to watch a film but fall asleep. I get up a few times in the night to wet Pete's mouth, all in all not a bad night.

I go home to cuddle with the grandkids, a few hours of normality, they ask lots of questions about Grampsy, bless them so hard, to know but not to see him, hard as we've always been truthful about what is happening.

Weirdly, his contact lenses are popping out quite regularly, most of the time, I've managed to be around and either popped them back in or put them into solution, one even popped out when he was having a poop, luckily the nurse put it back in for him, think Pete is going to have to start wearing his glasses more.

Another chat with the doctor about maybe going home, all it did was make Pete really grumpy. Cheryl did tell him not to die on her birthday, she didn't want to share her 40th with the first anniversary of his death (she was joking) bloody MND, keeping us all in limbo, even though Pete is trying to take back control, he's not having much luck.

Pete is drowsy, grumpy, has noisy breathing, is now dribbling, struggling to swallow, struggling to use his eye gaze, and has not pooped so needs a suppository and they say he may come home. I love this man so much, I miss him and he's still here.

Pete had a milkshake today, he couldn't drink/eat all of it but he did enjoy it, struggled to stay awake with visitors, even with the stories and laughter, but he fell asleep as soon as they walked out of the door, then he seemed to develop a cough, couldn't seem to clear it, not even with the cough assist.

He was hoisted and repositioned. I rubbed/patted his back to try to ease it, and continued to rub his back as he was turned, it helped a little but not much, he did manage a bit of curry and cheesecake (all made to a consistency he could cope with), but again that cough.

I left late, he was already asleep, coughing, grunting, and struggling. I was half expecting a call in the night, thankfully, it never came.

He had a crap night, he looked awful and sounded awful, they had given him different meds to try and help but nothing had worked, it brought tears to my eyes, but I couldn't let Pete see that, the last thing he needed was to get upset himself and then struggle even more, he couldn't even suck up his drink today.

Pete did manage to message Cheryl to wish her a happy birthday and to say he'd made it! His mum and sisters wanted to come to see him, I explained his breathing wasn't good, it was their choice, and they came anyway.

The doctor came in to listen to his chest, a definite deterioration, more calming and sedating meds and something to try and ease the cough, he managed to write, "Good, means I won't be going home," which made the doctor laugh.

He spent the afternoon coughing, napping and getting frustrated with the eye gaze, increased meds means he is struggling to use it, and struggling to communicate, he asked me to message his mates and the harem to explain why the lack of communication. I go home to peace and quiet, much needed, shitty, crap tough day.

Next few nights are spent at the hospice, Pete is struggling, he's frustrated at not being able to use the eye gaze properly and not being able to clear the cough, very restless at night, up and down with him, and his breathing sounds terrible (in my opinion) and he has a bit of double vision (no wonder he's struggling with the eye gaze).

Two of his harem came to visit him, and asked me to tell them that he maybe has a week to live!

Pete is on meds to help dry his secretions, so I took his contacts out and put his glasses on, maybe, this will help with the eye gaze. Aunty is coming to visit today, so I nip home for a shower and to meet her.

Macca (he was with Pete) called to say they'd tried to clear the crap from Pete's chest, it'd made him sick. I literally got off the phone with him and the doctor called. Pete was really sick and they were going to sedate him. I jumped in the van with Aunty and drove to the hospice, I'd only been gone and hour and all hell had broken loose!

He was very agitated, not what I was expecting, he was fighting the meds, and it took a good few hours to calm him, the doc kept popping in and out to check on him. I was holding his hand, and the TV seemed to agitate him, so I changed channels, and then he calmed.

I went to take his glasses off, and again that agitated him so I put them back on. I left the room, his breathing worsened and he became agitated, Doc said he possibly had 24 hours. How could it go from a week to literally nothing? Before he was fully sedated he indicated he didn't want anyone coming to see him.

I went out to the peace of the gardens and made calls to his family, then he changed his mind about his mum, so I called his brother and asked if he could bring her up, she spent a couple of hours with him before going home.

Macca and Andy came up, and took turns to sit with him or go to the family room. Liv and Tris came up for a while, Jay, Lola and Cheryl came, and said she was staying the night with me.

Phil was in Paris for work. Pete was now calm, fully sedated, could he hear us, I'd like to think so. I jumped out of bed every time he moaned or seemed distressed, finally, falling asleep around 5:30 am.

Pete never woke up again, his colour was ashen and his breathing was getting shallower, the nurse checked on him and said everything seemed fine. Macca and Andy were back, playing tag, one in with us, one in the family room.

Liv, Tris and Jay were back with Lola. I sat holding Pete's hand, Cheryl told him she was going to get something to eat, she'd barely left the room when I noticed Pete's chest was no longer moving. I asked Andy to go get Cheryl. I pressed the buzzer, not that anyone could do anything, he had the final bit of control, waiting for Cheryl to leave the room.

Just after midday on 24 August 2022, 19 months after his diagnosis (two years since my diagnosis) Pete's fight is finally over, he is free and at peace. My heart is broken, I've lost my best friend, my lover, my soul mate, but I'm glad he's no longer suffering.

I was asked which undertakers as they have no mortuary at the hospice. I blanked and panicked, had we discussed one, then remembered he wanted to go to the one his dad had used.

I spent a final few minutes with Pete, and then Cheryl and Jay cleared all his stuff. Cheryl brought me home. Andy called to say they were going up the pub, I made a few phone calls and then spent the afternoon/evening up the pub.

There was a little family altercation (of course there was), lots of tears, lots of drink, lots of stories and much laughter. I was fine till the undertaker called to say they had Pete, then I sobbed.

Phil arrived back from Paris around 6ish, he'd had a few tears on the train (bless him). Liv is holding it together remarkably well, she should be going to the reading festival (we'd got her tickets for Christmas). Cheryl exhausted goes home to tell the kids.

It's been a few days since Pete's passing, it seems like a lifetime, my sister slept over, so had a late night, which meant I actually slept and met my brother at the pub. Liv joined us after dropping Tris back home, she broke down in tears as soon as she walked into the pub.

Really had to nag Liv to pack for the reading festival, she should've gone yesterday, so hard for her, my sister eventually dropped her at the station as she went home. (Liv managed one night at the reading festival, then came home, and went back the next day to finish the festival). Donna popped in as I'd not answered her message.

Phil came over to sort the will and Pete's passport, and then took the van to be cleaned and ready for selling, Cheryl, Jay and the kids arrived (it's like a tag team, they don't want me to be on my own).

Macca popped in, he's struggling, he couldn't go into the house, luckily weather is nice so we can sit outside, he mentioned carrying Pete at the funeral, and said he wouldn't be able to do it.

I agreed, said he was too short anyway and Pete hadn't asked for anyone to carry him, from personal experience he knew how hard it was. Everyone left then Phil arrived, followed by Barb. I needed to go to the pub to sort out a little family issue. Barb and Donna came too, rude not to have a drink or two. After lots of tears this morning, feel strangely calm, almost like I can feel Pete around me.

Some many phone calls, lots of messages, cards, flowers, and so much love and support, my days are very up and down, but I'm coping, but everything is so strange. I had to take stuff back to the hospice, Cheryl and Lola came too, and we took gifts for the staff to show our appreciation, it was actually very cathartic.

I didn't go on the ward, I couldn't cope with it, lots of hugs from the lovely staff and I went to find the name of the rose bush. I sat many a time admiring, funnily enough, it was called *at peace,* very apt.

Phil is working away for a couple of weeks then he'll be coming to stay with me for a while, he'll be able to help sort stuff and I'm guessing keep an eye on me. Pete's death has been registered, and his bank account closed.

Cheryl and I, spent a couple of hours sorting his funeral, so thankful for his input, hopefully, I've got everything he asked for and I didn't have to really think about it too much. Very emotional day, feel so sad and alone, long to feel the comfort and safety of Pete's arms around me.

Test drove a car today, not in the frame of mind, but guess at some point I'll need to make a decision. Rose bushes arrived, made me feel very emotional, took one to Pete's mum, and promptly burst into tears, for goodness sake, need to pull myself together.

I try not to cry in front of anyone, especially the kids. Liv bless her, is emotional enough, she just wants her dad back, her proper dad, not the sick one. On top of all this emotion, we have a thunderstorm, I don't like them, never have, to be fair I did stand watching the lightning from the kitchen window, very brave for me, Liv came and checked I was all right, bless her.

I decided to take myself off to Kent for a few days to the tranquillity of my aunt, she lives in the middle of nowhere, Liv drove me down, and the flipping thunderstorm only went and followed us, I lay in bed watching the lightning bouncing over the fields.

Another reason for coming to Kent. Auntie's friend is taking Pete's service so it's an ideal opportunity to catch up and sort things out with him. I feel so at peace here, know its short-lived and I'll be returning to reality in a few days, just enjoying being cocooned for the time being, watching the birds, and rabbits in the field and listening to nothingness.

Such a great place to hide from reality. Got home in record time, considering the rubbish weather, and walked indoors. Pete's bed was still here, the eye gaze and his chair, such a stark reminder. Hopefully, we've found a home for his chair, one less thing once it's picked up, chase up about the other bits being picked up.

Still no info from the funeral directors, that's a bit worrying. Cheryl's down, so she chases them for me, I find I can deal with things on the phone but if it gets too challenging, I crack and cry, what a woose. So thankful for the kids and knowing they'll sort things for me.

Cheryl has also taken photos of a now very clean van, it's going on an auction site in the next day or so, luckily, Liv will be taking herself back to uni in London soon, so I'll have the use of her car. Spoke to Pete's mates about carrying him in the crem, they are willing and think it's a privilege. Everything still seems so unreal, like he is away and will be home anytime.

Liv drove herself to London (brave girl) to drop her stuff off at her uni digs, came back then I dropped them off at the train station, my brother and his wife came to see me, lovely to catch up. I tidy and clean. I'm wandering around like a lost soul. Is this what my life is going to be like? Then, I get a call to say the van has been sold and will be collected in a few days, I cry like a baby and take myself round to see Donna.

Cheryl and I go to see the funeral directors, time is ticking and nothing seems to have been done, they say they are too busy to see us, we stand out ground, so many things not confirmed that should've been, so many things we haven't seen and a deadline of today for printing!

Need to get the order of service sorted and the photos. The obituary website kept crashing, wrong hospice website, for goodness sake, frustrated, I took myself for a walk. Finally, everything is checked and in for printing, the website sorted and posted on FB phew, then a call to the florist to get Liv some sunflowers throws up a few issues.

They were trying to get red orchids, why? I've no idea. I wanted white orchids and red roses (big sigh of relief from them), even *dad* which should've been in red and white (Arsenal colours) was wrong, so glad we phoned for something else, can't imagine what we would've ended up with on the day. I'm exhausted and emotionally drained.

The bed is being collected, Donna is popping around to be with me, actually, I was okay, very strange seeing an empty space which had been occupied since we'd moved in, hoovered and cleaned up the area, which didn't feel so bad. Next, the van goes, again not as emotional as I thought, they were here for six minutes, now I have the money to buy myself a car, if only I can decide on what car I want.

I'm struggling to sleep, feel exhausted, my body is aching and my head is all over the place. I'm having my chemo curls cut off, it's time to sort my hair out. Phil is back, at least, I'll have company in the house.

Liv and Tris are home, we're off to the pub to meet the boys before the funeral and check they know who's where for carrying Pete. Some people were at the bar, some sat around the table, half a pint of beer seemed to fly off the table throwing beer on the seat, everyone just looking at each other, was Pete making his presence known, who knows, made us all laugh.

Lovely to see everyone, very emotional, now I just want to miss tomorrow, go to sleep and wake up the day after, if only life was that simple.

There is a chill in the air, the sun is out. I drop Liv, Tris and Phil into town as I head off for my blood test (yes life goes on, it doesn't stop for death), not even a bruise this time, result. I return home to an empty quiet house, I can't settle, wandering, and fidgeting.

Cheryl, Jay and kids arrive with food and drink, then Liv, Tris and Phil from town. How can a day feel so long, I guess that's what happens when I fulfil Pete's wishes, the last funeral of the day on a Friday!

We amuse ourselves with senseless games, body press-ups on a chair, timing each other, really, but it makes us all laugh, which is much needed. Pete's choice of attire for the funeral is bright colours, football tops, running colours, and no black. I'm wearing a pink Arsenal football top.

I have a big issue with my hair, an SOS call to my hairdresser and she comes to sort it out, bless her (stopping getting ready herself). Pete's mum and brother arrive as they are coming in the car with us.

Pete comes home, and the flowers look lovely, I cry. Liv cries, Joshua cries, and Cheryl thinks his wicker coffin looks like a laundry basket (to be fair it does), which makes us all laugh, it's time to get the show on the road. His running club have a guard of honour by the pub, which makes me cry again, but I quickly compose myself.

For some reason, we sit for a while behind bushes before going to where we get out, those carrying Pete are briefed, and

I'm walking beside him for one last time, seating arrangements seem to be in chaos.

Cheryl goes to make sure we all have seats, very confusing, we start to walk in, and everyone follows behind, losing the kids. Phil has to step in, how can things be so chaotic? Beautiful service, Cheryl gave a reading, which she stumbled over, she did announce to everyone I'd given her the wrong one and she'd only just got the right one.

Yep, I had, did cause a laugh. I gave a reading, looking over at Pete as I read it, his childhood friend Mike said some beautiful, very emotional words as did one of his sisters-in-law, and we left him a miniature bottle of vodka. Graham gave a fantastic service, Pete even wrote a speech to be read out, having to have the last word right to the end.

The last song is dedicated to me, and that's when I crack, I've managed to keep it together right up to the end, the song is playing, are we supposed to get up to leave or not, no one seems to be indicating anything.

Graham eventually steps in and starts people moving out. I get up to go, Liv has an absolute meltdown, sobbing and crying in my arms, not wanting to leave her dad (the first funeral she has ever been to).

Pete's brother comes and takes her from my arms, my heart is breaking for her. So many people, so little time, we are whisked off to the pub for the wake, there is nowhere to park, we are dropped off at the bottom of the car park. As Pete's wishes, Cheryl and Phil go around giving raffle tickets to people, the only way we could come up with to let everyone have a drink on Pete. (he also wanted his mates to have money to buy a few rounds on him).

Phil gave a speech and a toast to Pete, there were many tears, many stories, much laughter and even more drinks, so many people, I have no idea how many (someone reckoned there were around 500), some I knew, some I didn't.

Someone asked Donna what we were celebrating, and when she was told it was a wake, she was mortified. Our niece was asked to leave the pub and banned, almost at the end of the evening, why? She'd helped herself to a drink from the bar, Pete would've been proud of her and laughed.

Pete would have loved it, we did him proud, a true celebration of his life, just as he wanted it.

Now, it's time for me to face my cancer, I no longer have Pete to hide behind.